To the memory of
Roger Andersen

Contents

The author and series editors

Catherine Wallace is a lecturer in Education in the Department of English for Speakers of Other Languages at the University of London Institute of Education. She has long experience of language teaching and teacher training in ESL and EFL, both in Britain and overseas. Her professional interests include, as well as the teaching of reading, early literacy and cross-cultural communication.

Christopher N. Candlin is Professor of Linguistics in the School of English and Linguistics at Macquarie University, Sydney, and Director of the National Centre for English Language Teaching and Research, having previously been Professor of Applied Linguistics and Director of the Centre for Language in Social Life at the University of Lancaster. He also co-founded and directed the Institute for English Language Education at Lancaster, where he worked on issues in in-service education for teachers.

Henry Widdowson is Professor of English for Speakers of Other Languages at the University of London Institute of Education, having previously been Lecturer in Applied Linguistics at the University of Edinburgh. Before that, he worked on materials development and teacher education as a British Council English Language Officer in Sri Lanka and Bangladesh.

Through work with The British Council, The Council of Europe, and other agencies, both Editors have had extensive and varied experience of language teaching, teacher education, and curriculum development overseas, and both contribute to seminars, conferences, and professional journals.

Introduction

Reading

This book considers reading and learning to read as a social, interactive process as much as a personal and private activity. Its aim is not therefore to offer a comprehensive account of reading research or of teaching approaches, but rather to focus on those aspects of research and practice which have a social, interactive orientation.

Section One opens by introducing some key terms central to the emphasis of the book. I then consider, in turn, the social role of the reader, the social context of reading, and the social nature of meanings within texts. The section concludes with a discussion of the factors which affect the reader's engagement with the text during the reading process.

Section Two considers the perspective of the second language reader in the learning process: first it examines the nature of learning to read and learner readers, in particular the roles and purposes of the second language reader; then the selection of texts for the classroom and classroom procedures are discussed. The concluding unit of Section Two centres on texts and classroom procedures which, it is argued, might offer learners greater critical insight into the ways texts and reading processes are socially constructed.

Section Three follows the same general progression as the first two sections, by looking in turn at the reader, the text, and classroom procedures. It is designed to help teachers relate principle to practice through a range of tasks, suitable for different proficiency levels, which can be carried out in the course of typical language classes.

I should like to thank Henry Widdowson for his time and patience, and the interesting debates we had about areas of this book—not all of them by any means resolved! Thanks are due too, to Chris Candlin for his very constructive help in clarifying and challenging many points in early versions of my text. Finally I am particularly indebted to my colleagues and students in the English Language Teaching Department at Thames Valley University (formerly Ealing College of Higher Education) who have over the years helped to shape many of the ideas in this book.

Catherine Wallace

Language Teaching: A Scheme for Teacher Education

The purpose of this scheme of books is to engage language teachers in a process of continual professional development. We have designed it so as to guide teachers towards the critical appraisal of ideas and the informed application of these ideas in their own classrooms. The scheme provides the means for teachers to take the initiative themselves in pedagogic planning. The emphasis is on critical enquiry as a basis for effective action.

We believe that advances in language teaching stem from the independent efforts of teachers in their own classrooms. This independence is not brought about by imposing fixed ideas and promoting fashionable formulas. It can only occur where teachers, individually or collectively, explore principles and experiment with techniques. Our purpose is to offer guidance on how this might be achieved.

The scheme consists of three sub-series of books covering areas of enquiry and practice of immediate relevance to language teaching and learning. Sub-series 1 focuses on areas of *language knowledge*, with books linked to the conventional levels of linguistic description: pronunciation, vocabulary, grammar, and discourse. Sub-series 2 (of which this present volume forms a part) focuses on different *modes of behaviour* which realize this knowledge. It is concerned with the pedagogic skills of speaking, listening, reading, and writing. Sub-series 3 focuses on a variety of *modes of action* which are needed if this knowledge and behaviour is to be acquired in the operation of language teaching. The books in this sub-series have to do with such topics as syllabus design, the content of language courses, and aspects of methodology and evaluation.

This sub-division of the field is not meant to suggest that different topics can be dealt with in isolation. On the contrary, the concept of a scheme implies making coherent links between all these different areas of enquiry and activity. We wish to emphasize how their integration formalizes the complex factors present in any teaching process. Each book, then, highlights a particular topic, but also deals contingently with other issues, themselves treated as focal in other books in the series. Clearly, an enquiry into a mode of behaviour like speaking, for example, must also refer to aspects of language knowledge which it realizes. It must also connect to modes of action which can be directed at developing this behaviour in learners. As elements of the whole scheme, therefore, books cross-refer both within and across the different sub-series.

This principle of cross-reference which links the elements of the scheme is also applied to the internal design of the different inter-related books within it. Thus, each book contains three sections, which, by a combination of text and task, engage the reader in a principled enquiry into ideas and practices. The first section of each book makes explicit those theoretical ideas which bear on the topic in question. It provides a conceptual framework for those sections which follow. Here the text has a mainly *explanatory* function, and the tasks serve to clarify and consolidate the points raised. The second section shifts the focus of attention to how the ideas from Section One relate to activities in the classroom. Here the text is concerned with *demonstration*, and the tasks are designed to get readers to evaluate suggestions for teaching in reference both to the ideas from Section One and also to their own teaching experience. In the third section this experience is projected into future work. Here the set of tasks, modelled on those in Section Two, are designed to be carried out by the reader as a combination of teaching techniques and action research in the actual classroom. It is this section that renews the reader's contact with reality: the ideas expounded in Section One and linked to pedagogic practice in Section Two are now to be systematically *tested out* in the process of classroom teaching.

If language teaching is to be a genuinely professional enterprise, it requires continual experimentation and evaluation on the part of practitioners whereby in seeking to be more effective in their pedagogy they provide at the same time—and as a corollary—for their own continuing education. It is our aim in this scheme to promote this dual purpose.

Christopher N. Candlin
Henry Widdowson

Explanation
The nature of reading

1   Reading and readers

1.1   What reading means

The most important resource that any potential reader possesses, whether reading in a first or any other language, is an awareness of the way in which we use language. For reading is above all to do with language. There are two things which we all know about language: first that we use it for a purpose; second that it only makes sense in context, that is as part of a larger text or in a situation. With this in mind, let us look at examples of reading behaviour in several different settings.

▶   TASK 1

What reading purposes might the people in the following situations have?

1 A man on an underground station raises his eyes to a computer printout message displayed on a screen.

2 A three-year-old child on her father's knee turns the pages of a picture book.

3 A student in a library gazes intently at a textbook, occasionally making notes.

Clearly the purposes of these three people are all different, though each might be described as 'reading'. We see that purpose and physical setting are linked in that we cannot identify a likely purpose for the activity without some knowledge of the setting. For example, in the first situation we need to know that many London Underground stations now have computerized information about train services. And just as reading itself will mean different things in different contexts, so will the question 'Can you read?'

▶   TASK 2

Consider what the question 'Can you read this?' might mean in the following situations.

1 An adult is having a sight test at an optician's and is asked to read a list of words.

2 A child in class is shown a flash card with the word 'here' on it by her teacher.

3 An Islamic religious leader asks a congregation of boys to read aloud the Koran.

4 The owner of a new computer asks an experienced friend about the instructions in the manual.

In each case we will need to widen our understanding of context to consider not just the physical setting of the activity but who is speaking to whom and in what set of circumstances. Asked by optician of client, the question 'Can you read?' in the first situation will be taken to mean 'Are you able to *identify* the words on the card?', that is has the client the physical ability to see the words. In the second situation the teacher is likely to mean 'Can you *decode* this text?', that is read it aloud, rather than attribute a meaning to the word—hardly possible in the case of a word such as 'here', especially when presented outside a sentence context. One of the difficulties which young children may have, in fact, is not knowing whether an ability to read is supposed to also involve an *understanding* of what is read. In the third situation the expected reading behaviour may not even involve decoding—that is the ability to relate written symbols to sound, for in some religious contexts texts may be learned and recited by rote. Readers are able to recognize sections of these texts according to such features as the position of print on the page and the headings. They would not be able to render the same section aloud if encountered in a different textual context. We might call this style of reading 'recitation'. Finally, if we consider a likely meaning for the question 'Can you read this?' in the fourth situation, we might want to say that 'read' could be substituted by 'interpret'. Here we are talking about the need to work out the meaning of a written text with the purpose of being able to take some kind of action as a result.

Unless otherwise stated, I shall use 'reading' in this final sense throughout this book. Reading as interpreting means reacting to a written text as a piece of communication; in other words, we assume some communicative intent on the writer's part which the reader has some purpose in attempting to understand.

In short, the way we perceive reading behaviour is linked to different reader purposes which, in turn, are linked to situational context and also to social expectations, for example what kind of reading behaviour is expected in classrooms, families, or particular religious settings. The social dimension of both written texts and reading behaviour will be discussed more fully in 3, 4, and 5. First let us look more generally at what it means to be a reader in contemporary societies.

1.2 What being a reader means

Reading is so much a part of daily life for those of us who live in literate communities that much of the time we hardly consider either the purposes or processes involved. We take the activity for granted, much as we do with listening and speaking (less so, perhaps, in the case of writing). Certainly, there are poor readers—even non-readers—in literate societies, and many manage to develop strategies which compensate, in part, for minimal reading ability. Nonetheless, urban technological societies operate on the premise that their members can read. For instance they are expected to be able to read the names of political parties and their candidates in order to exercise the right to vote; to understand the words which follow 'caution' on medications and household products, and to understand the purpose of the reminder to pay a telephone bill and the accompanying threat of disconnection on failure to do so.

Many of these assumptions are, of course, misplaced and we have all, at times, been caught out by our failure to read with sufficient attention even when the material closely affects our interests. It should be added that the reader is not always at fault—some material is simply unreadable. However, where failure is due, at least partly, to our own inadequacies as readers, this need hardly surprise us in view of the sheer volume of print with which we are daily bombarded, much of it uninvited or unwelcome. A typical example of this is the advertising material which has recently come to be very appropriately described as 'junk mail'.

Both our immediate response and the eventual outcome of reading will be variable. Experienced readers make judgements during any reading activity about the degree of care and attention which the material warrants. In the real world, effective reading means a flexible and appropriate response to the material in hand, and this is always guided by the reader's purpose; it means that readers are aware that they have options, including the option to give up. How often, for instance, do we read a newspaper article all the way through rather than just glancing at the headlines and the first couple of paragraphs?

In other words, our day-to-day reading behaviour is highly selective. Just as we filter spoken messages in deciding what to attend to, so do we filter written messages. And even when we commit ourselves to a full reading, that reading will still be selective, some parts being read with greater care than others.

▶   TASK 3

As far as possible, recollect all the reading material which you have encountered during the day, including things like letters, print on bottles or packets, and street signs.

1 How did you respond in each case (for example, cursory read, careful scrutiny, or by immediately discarding it?)

2 What did you do as a result of the reading activity (for example, produce some kind of writing, reflect on the implications of what you read, turn on the TV?)

It may be, for instance, that your response to a request for money from a charity was a casual glance followed by putting it aside to be dealt with later, while a bill demanded immediate attention. The reasons for our responses to and the results of any reading activity are likely to depend on factors such as conflicting demands on our time, attention, and energy and, in particular, on our *purpose* in reading any particular text.

1.3 Reading purpose

Any mode of language, whether it be listening, speaking, reading, or writing may be used to serve immediate needs, to learn from, or to give us pleasure in language for its own sake. An important feature which reading also shares with other modes of language use is its role in social interaction. This important area is considered more fully in 3, 4, and 5. For the moment let us look at some of the more personal reasons for reading.

Reading for survival

We might call some kinds of reading in response to our environment 'reading for survival'. Indeed some reading is almost literally a matter of life and death—for example a 'stop' sign for a motorist. Survival reading serves immediate needs or wishes. Obvious examples are 'ladies', 'gentlemen', and 'exit'. Less obvious examples given to me by students recently arrived in Britain are 'off peak' (indicating that a travel ticket can only be used outside the rush-hour) and 'way out' rather than the more familiar 'exit'.

▶ TASK 4

1 Can you think of other examples of what I have called survival reading, in whatever language, which relate to your own daily life?

2 How are we able to identify survival reading for any individual? For example what might count as survival reading for:
   – a young child
   – a factory worker
   – a tourist?

Young children, for instance, tend to feel that things like ice creams and hamburgers are, if not essential, at least important to their well-being. In fact it has been found that children from all social backgrounds very readily acquire an understanding of print, related to the ways they perceive their day-to-day needs and interests, from such sources as TV, advertising, and street signs. This is sometimes called 'environmental print'. For other social groups such as parents survival reading might involve the ability to read instructions on baby food and safety regulations on toys.

Reading for learning

As well as a means of finding out information on a strictly utilitarian basis—reading for survival—reading serves the wider role of extending our general knowledge of the world. Much day-to-day reading is for this purpose of learning. Moreover we may want not so much to learn something new as to remind ourselves about half-known facts or vaguely formulated opinions. For instance, as I write this book I move between the text I am creating and key sources in order to support, consolidate, and clarify my ideas.

One might expect reading for learning to be exclusively school related. In fact, while a good deal of reading to support learning clearly takes place in academic contexts—and I discuss the nature of some of these in Section Two—there are also many kinds of reading activities sanctioned and supported by educational institutions which arguably have little to do with acquiring facts or opinions. The function of some of these activities is what Goodman (1984) has called 'ritualistic'. One example of this would be those situations when readers read aloud a text either individually to the teacher or to the whole class with, as may become evident on questioning, little understanding of its content. Particularly where English is being learned as a second or foreign language 'language practice' may take the form of 'reading round the class'. This kind of reading might be said to have a 'display' function rather than offering evidence of learning or reflection.

Reading for pleasure

While reading for survival involves an immediate response to a situation and reading for learning is also goal orientated, albeit in a rather different way, reading for pleasure is done for its own sake—we don't have to do it. This point may be lost on children in school where literature, originally written primarily to offer enjoyment, is required reading for examinations. Educational practices tend to neglect the pleasure principle, producing young learners of the kind quoted by Clark (1976) who, although already a fluent reader, expressed the view that the purpose of learning to read was 'so that you can stop'! And if readers do not read for pleasure in their mother-tongue they are very unlikely to do so in a second or foreign language. An important by-product of reading for pleasure in any language is fluency. This can create a vicious circle. Unless a reader gains fluency, that is speed and ease of reading, the reading of any material for whatever purpose is likely to be tedious. This, in turn, decreases motivation to read anything other than essential 'survival' material—the minimum required to function in school or the workplace—and fluency never gets a chance to develop.

2 Written language: text and discourse

Just as there are different ways of looking at what people do, and why, when they read, so there are different ways of looking at written language. It is possible to consider written language from two broad perspectives: we can look at features of the product as we see it in written or printed form, or we can look at the underlying sets of meanings which the writer brings into play in the course of producing the text, and which the reader, in turn, processes in the course of interpreting it. We might call these perspectives following, for example, Alderson and Urquhart (1984), a *product* dimension and a *process* dimension. This distinction between product and process can be linked to a view of reading as *text* or as *discourse* respectively, an idea which will be developed in the course of this book. For the moment we might describe text as the output of a writer which can be recorded and studied, while a discourse approach to reading focuses less on the text as product and more on the reader's process of constructing meaning from it. Here we will consider each perspective in turn.

2.1 Reading and text

'A text is the verbal record of a communicative act' (Brown and Yule 1983:6). Halliday (Halliday and Hasan 1985:10) in a similar definition describes text as language that is functional, that is which is 'doing some job' such as persuading us to buy a product or conveying New Year's greetings. In line with these functional definitions, I shall be using the term 'text' to mean any chunk of written language which carries a whole meaning and is describable by some term such as 'warning', 'novel', or 'letter'.

One way of looking at texts is to see them as the physical manifestation of language, the data the reader works with to construct meaning, which consists of actual marks on the page. These marks include the whole range of graphic features which follow generally agreed conventions about the nature of the writing system and are thus communicative. So, for example, colons and speech bubbles are part of texts, but ink blots are not.

There are also agreed ways in which chunks of language longer than words or phrases connect in order to create unified pieces of language rather than mere strings of sentences. In the following sections I shall look first at some salient features of the writing system and then at features of connected text.

The writing system

Let us first look at some of the difficulties of form and meaning which the English writing system presents, particularly to someone beginning reading in English who is coming to the language as a non-native speaker and who may be familiar with a different writing system.

The English writing system is frequently charged with being chaotic on the grounds that correspondences between sound and written symbol are much less consistent than in languages such as Spanish, Urdu, Hindi, and Arabic, where there is a clearer one-to-one correspondence between the flow of speech and the sequence of marks on the page. It so happens that English has its own regularities which are simply rather different from the more fully phonetic languages with which it tends to be compared. These regularities will be discussed below.

The lack of a predictable sound–symbol correspondence in English has an immediate implication for learner readers. They cannot initially make the necessary connection between the language they hear and the language they see in print. For example, we might take a situation where the learner has the word 'danger' in his or her oral repertoire but may not immediately relate this to the same word in printed form. He or she might expect the word to be pronounced /dængə/, especially if taught by a phonic method which focuses on the decoding of printed symbol to sound.

► ## TASK 5

Yasmeen, literate in Urdu and in the early stages of learning to read in English, is reading aloud to her teacher a text which describes 'signing on' (registering) at the Job Centre. What expectations about the English writing system are revealed by Yasmeen's comments? Have you had similar responses from your own students?

Yasmeen: 'I went to sign on.'
Teacher: What does it mean 'to sign on'?
Yasmeen: Yes, I know 'sign' but spelling wrong!
Teacher: No, it's spelt like that.
Yasmeen: 'g'?
Teacher: You know, English spelling is very funny.
Yasmeen: Yes, very funny. S–i–g–n. (*attempts to sound out the letters phonetically*) Too hard!

Yasmeen knew the spoken form of the word 'sign' from having frequently heard phrases such as 'sign your name' and 'to sign on at the Job Centre'. She was frustrated by the fact that she could not readily predict the features of the written form from the spoken form because the English writing system is much less phonetically based than Urdu script.

What may help learners like Yasmeen is an understanding that the consistency demonstrated by English is best described not as between letters and sounds, but as lying *within* the visual or graphic system itself. There are two major ways through which readers may make these visual connections in texts. First, they may use grammatical cues. These are consistently conveyed in the writing system. For example, the final '-ed' in regular past tense verbs is quite consistent across the words 'walked', 'painted', and 'loved' though it is pronounced differently in keeping with its different phonetic environment. The reader recognizes these three words as grammatically similar not through the way they are pronounced, which varies, but through the '-ed' ending, which is graphically invariable.

The English writing system also reveals similarities and differences connected with meaning. For instance, words that have similar visual configurations are likely to be semantically related; thus we relate 'site' to 'situation', 'cite' to 'citation', 'writing' to 'writer', 'system' to 'systematic', and 'sign' to 'signify' and 'signature'. Conversely, as Stubbs (1980) points out, phonetically similar but visually different words are usually semantically distinct, for example 'rite', 'rights', and 'writer'.

▶ # TASK 6

Consider how these words could be grouped using visual information.

*hole   manhole   site   situation   whole   wholly
whole-hearted   holy   witch   which   witch-hunt   sight
short-sighted   unsightly   cite   citation   whichever   holey
holiness*

We see that the resulting groups, classified using visual criteria alone, offer us semantic sets, that is groups of words linked in terms of meaning. In short, we *see* not *hear* the relationship between 'site' and 'situation', 'nation' and 'nationality', and 'cite' and 'citation'. So much so that when newly coined words adopt a phonetic principle rather than one which maintains the semantic link with existing words we do a 'double take' as I did on first encountering the unfamiliar word 'travolator' above a moving walkway at Heathrow Airport (since changed, I note, to the expected form 'travelator').

It should be said that one needs to be cautious in claiming that the semantic basis for identifying words is entirely regular and predictable. There are some exceptions, for example, 'palace' and 'palatial', and 'speak' and 'speech'. None the less learners confronted with the English writing system will generally do better to use visual similarity with known words rather than sound as a basis when attempting to identify new words. It will be evident, as Stubbs (1980) points out, that the English writing system helps those who are already literate more than those who are embarking on learning to read. Inexperienced readers need considerable access to print before they can begin spontaneously to make relevant connections between words with visual similarities. However, for experienced readers who speak a language related to English, words may be more readily recognized in written than in spoken contexts. In the latter there may be difficulties, due to variable stress, with semantically related items such as 'pho'tography', ''photograph' and 'photo'graphic'.

Features of connected text

As well as being aware of patterning at word level, readers need to be able to make sense of connected text. When we encounter texts, whether written or spoken, we recognize them as pieces of communication rather than mere strings of words or sentences. This is because of the way parts of a text relate to each other to create a meaningful whole, and the whole takes on meaning from its situational and cultural context. It is possible to look at texts in three different ways: (1) in terms of their *formal features*, that is, at ways features of the grammatical system are used to link sentences or paragraphs; (2) in terms of their *propositional meaning*, that is how ideas or concepts are expressed and related to each other, and (3) in terms of their *communicative function*, both the ways in which sections of a text can be interpreted in relation to other sections and of the function of any text as a whole.

▶ ## TASK 7

1 Which of these four samples of writing would you consider a text?

2 What kind of criteria can one use in deciding whether a sample might or might not be counted a text?

Sample A
Yesterday's decision also means a reprieve for the associated Blackburn-Hellifield line. Latest estimates suggest the bill will be between £2 million and £3 million. He was concerned at the hardship facing local people. It will now look at ways of cutting costs.

Sample B
The boats are on the water. The men have the nets in the boats. Off they go. The men go off in the boats. They go off to fish.

Sample C
Women on their own cannot really have a life because of the world. When they do get a chance to go out people think they are going out just for men. But they are not really going out for men. They get tired sitting in the house. They get very depressed and frightened. They want to go out for company.

Sample D

Look at these two men! One is very tall and thin. He has long hair. He is Mr Diab. The second man is short and fat. He is carrying a black bag. His name is Mr Haddad. Mr Diab is not carrying a bag. He is holding a small book in his right hand and he is showing it to Mr Haddad. They are not walking now. They are standing near the traffic lights.

Although the samples are all extracted from larger stretches of writing, which include visuals in the case of samples B, C, and D, we can still make some sort of sense of them as they stand. First, all the samples consist of strings of well-formed sentences. However in each case there is some difficulty in the way the sentences relate to each other in terms of form, meaning, and function. Let us consider each in turn.

One term which is used to describe certain formal features in texts is 'cohesion'. Cook (1989), in *Discourse* in this Scheme, gives a detailed account of cohesion, describing as 'cohesive devices' the formal links between sentences and clauses. Here we shall take just one example of a cohesive device, personal pronouns such as 'it', 'he', and 'they'. These function in texts as *referring expressions*, that is they refer us to other parts of the surrounding text or they may refer outside the text to people, things, or events which are understood to be present in the situation. In sample A we see that we have a problem, for we are unable to find a referent for 'he' in line 3 or 'it' in line 4. In sample B there is also a problem with pronouns—here it is their absence which strikes us. For in most kinds of text a pronoun necessarily replaces a previous noun where we are referring to the same person or thing. For example, if I say 'John hit the ball. Then John ran away', in most situations we would assume that we are talking of two different men or boys called John. The formal rule is simple: if the same person is being referred to, substitute with the appropriate pronoun, in this case 'he'. In sample B, this rule is partially broken so that in the second sentence the expected substitution of 'them' for 'boats' does not occur. Morever, when 'they' *is* used in the third sentence, it turns out to be ambiguous, so we are not sure whether it refers to 'boats' or 'men'.

We do not simply recognize forms in texts—we recognize the propositional links which they signal. This is the difficulty with sample C. Amna, in the early stages of learning to read in English, spontaneously queried 'What means "they"?' on its first occurrence in the text. Her confusion was understandable, for it is difficult for a very early reader who is reading hesitatingly to make the connection between 'they' and its referent 'women on their own'. The problem is not merely a formal one—of finding the appropriate referent by relating a third person plural pronoun to a plural noun phrase. There is also a conceptual difficulty. Amna understood the concept of reference in principle—hence her search in the text. She offered as referents first 'child' (there was a picture of the woman who is telling the story, with her child, alongside the text) and then the word 'life' towards the end of the preceding sentence. The meaning difficulty here is that 'they' refers to 'women on their own', an abstract concept not represented by any characters in the story or in the accompanying picture. This suggests that it is not so much linguistic form on its own which creates difficulty for early learners as the way in which form relates to meaning and the fact that this relationship is not one-to-one (see Wallace 1987). In short, sample C is a legitimate text, cohesive to an experienced reader but difficult for a beginner.

Sample D creates yet another kind of difficulty. It is entirely cohesive, with pronouns relating clearly and unambiguously to preceding nouns. Our unease here is of a different kind. We cannot see what the communicative function of each individual sentence is in relation to the next. What is the function of the sentence 'Mr Diab is not carrying a bag'? We do not usually make negative statements simply to mark the absence of activity. I would be unlikely for instance to say or write, apropos of nothing in particular, 'I am not wearing silk pyjamas'. Moreover, how are we supposed to relate this negative statement to the positive one which follows: 'He is holding a small book in his right hand and he is showing it to Mr Haddad'? The nature of the difficulty is not so much a matter of cohesion as of coherence.

While the principle of cohesion operates to allow us to make propositional links in texts, our understanding of a text's coherence is achieved, even in the absence of cohesion, if we are also able to make functional links, for example to understand why statement B might follow statement A in:

A: The Director has resigned!
B: We'll open the champagne!

Here there are no cohesive markers such as coordination or referring pronouns. Nonetheless, it is possible to relate the function of the second sentence to that of the first. Indeed, each takes on a particular force in relation to the other. This example also makes it clear that coherence is dependent on a reader's or listener's ability to draw on relevant knowledge of the world, related to who the Director is, the attitude to him or her of speaker and addressee, and the occasions on which champagne is drunk. The nature of this knowledge of the world is discussed in 5.

Our understanding of a text's coherence is achieved not only through our ability to relate its parts to each other but also through the way in which we are able to ascribe a function to the text as a whole. What job is it doing? Of course, those of us familiar with language teaching material will immediately recognize the job that Sample D is doing. It is teaching English. In the same way Sample B is teaching reading, and is typical of certain reading books for children which break the normal rules of cohesion. Sample C is taken from a book written by an adult literacy student for other adult learners. In the case of Sample A, I simply took random sentences from the same news article. It should be added however that even here most readers will be willing to do quite a bit of interpretative work on the text before conceding that there are problems. This is in line with one principle mentioned in **1.1**, namely our expectation that language makes sense in context. Thus, when presented with a fragment of text, readers work hard to reconstruct a possible context from which it might have been drawn.

In conclusion, readers are helped in their interpretation of texts both by their knowledge of the principles of word formation and cohesion, and by their ability to attribute an appropriate communicative function to texts and parts of texts. Another factor which contributes to the interpretation of texts is the reader's familiarity with the discourses which are embedded in them. We shall look in detail at the nature of discourse in **2.2**.

2.2 Reading and discourse

In this book I shall use the term 'discourse' to describe the meaning which the reader constructs from the text during the reading process. It has been argued (see for example, Fairclough 1989) that there is not just a single discourse but a number of discourses which can be recovered by a reader from any text. These discourses are essentially social rather than personal and individual in that they relate to social practices and beliefs; in other words, they are ways of talking or writing about persons, places, events, or phenomena which relate to conventional beliefs or ways of doing things which are, in turn, associated with a society's key institutions. For example, there are conventional ways of talking or writing about phenomena such as dating, public schools, or family pets related to the social institutions of marriage, education, and the family.

Discourses typically reflect differences of power between the members of different social groups; for example, ways of talking about the roles of men and women in both the family and the workplace frequently indicate a less powerful position for women. Thus, we tend to talk of 'man and wife' rather than 'woman and husband'.

So deep-rooted are the assumptions which discourses reflect that readers are likely to see discourses as unexceptional as long as they come from the same social group as the writer and share broadly similar social experiences and values.

▶   TASK 8

Below is an extract from a reading book designed for British children who speak English as their mother tongue.

1 Is it possible to identify discourses in the text related to typical ways of describing male and female roles or social class roles?

2 Would these discourses be similarly presented in comparable texts in other cultural contexts with which you are familiar?

My Dad came home from work.
"Stop that noise,"
he said to Lennox.
"Lizzie," he said, "I want my tea.
I'm a working man.
I want three fried eggs.
I've been working all day
for the lot of you."
"Working all day?" said Mum.
"What about all those tea-breaks?
You have at least two every hour."

(*Gilroy 1975:7*)

Kress (1985) suggests that we can be made aware of the discourses contained within a text by asking ourselves *why* the topic is being written about, *how* the topic is being written about, and—most importantly—*what other ways* of writing about the topic there are. The last is important in that, simply because discourses are related to institutions the nature of which we rarely challenge, we may simply not have thought of what other ways of writing, or talking, about a particular topic are available to us.

▶ TASK 9

The text extract overleaf is taken from an article published in a British newspaper in Summer 1989. The headline was 'The blame that Spain must share'. (The names of people and places have been changed.) Consider:

1 Why is this topic being written about?

2 How is the topic being written about?

3 What other ways of writing about the topic are there?

ROBBIE IS NOT REALLY A LAGER lout. He has been turned into one. He lives at home with his parents in a rather sleepy market town in Somerset. He's neat, quiet. He's got a job.

He's an enthusiastic supporter of his cricket club and his idea of a night out is a dance with his girlfriend who was a bit upset he'd gone on holiday without her.

All of which makes the sight of him crumpled in a drunken heap among the cigarette ends on the floor of the Los Santos Bar at 2.30 a.m. so depressing.

Why is it you English behave like this? asked the bar's proprietor Jose Torres as we dragged Robbie out on to the pavement, spewing curses at everyone, before he recovered enough to lurch into the nearest disco.

A hypocritical question for a Spaniard to ask. The Spanish wring their hands and rightfully complain about the shameless excesses of British youth; excesses which have not gone away, despite their disappearance from the news, excesses that this week in Magalluf, Mallorca, caused the murder of young waiter Juan Sanchez.

We should be ashamed. But so, too, should the Spanish. For it is their ruthless and cynical exploitation of young tourists, pouring alcohol down their albeit willingly open throats, that has turned a potential problem into a disaster.

The Spanish have, whether they like it or not, created a factory for lager louts. Right across the Balearics and along the Costas they have nurtured a climate where drunken outrageous behaviour is almost inevitable. Drink is so available, so ridiculously cheap.

The reason why the topic has been chosen is fairly clear: the behaviour of the British abroad has once again attracted criticism. The text aims to explain and defend their behaviour. More interesting is the second question—the way the topic is handled, in other words the nature of the discourses selected by the writer. He draws on discourses about 'Britishness' and 'foreignness' which are set in opposition to each other by means of the kinds of language selected to talk about each. On the one hand the language used to talk about Robbie, the prototype young Englishman in the text, conveys decency, peace, and respectability ('sleepy market town', 'cricket club', 'girlfriend') while, on the other hand, the language used to describe the Spanish suggests dishonesty, unreliability, and hypocrisy ('ruthless', 'wring hands', 'cynical'). The significance of the language selected becomes more apparent when we consider the third question, i.e. what other ways of writing about the topic are there? Imagine, for instance, if the detailed description of Robbie, with which the text opens, had been of the young Spanish waiter who was murdered instead; or if, in the description of Robbie, certain lexical replacements were made so the text read 'he's a keen supporter of his *local football team*'. Moreover, it is not just lexical but syntactic features which offer evidence for the unequal treatment of the participants in this text. For instance the verbs describing Robbie tend to be either stative, for example, 'to be' and 'to have', or in the passive voice, suggesting overall a lack of responsibility for events, while those describing the Spanish are activity verbs, for example, 'to complain', 'to pour alcohol', 'to create'. Indeed, it is possible to argue that certain ways of talking about foreigners are institutionalized in the popular press in Britain.

Discourses are not just socially determined; they are culture specific. Ways of talking about foreigners, husbands, wives, and children will vary from one cultural group to another, whether, for instance, defined by class, nation, or gender. And because discourses relate to particular social practices, attitudes, and beliefs which the writer expects the reader to share, or at least to be familiar with, the reader from a different socio-cultural background may find the meaning of even apparently simple texts obscure. Thus, some of my students had difficulty in interpreting the text in Task 10. They had noticed it on the London Underground and had therefore encountered it in its immediate physical context. They had also realized it was an advertisement for British Telecom. They remained mystified however, largely because of their lack of familiarity with culture-specific features of the discourses in the text.

▶ **TASK 10**

Look at the advertisement below. In what way are the discourses in it culture-specific?

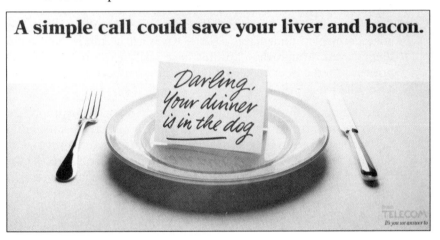

First, of course, there are difficulties to do with the language itself—what we might call text-based difficulties. An example here is the way in which two commonly used expressions, 'save your bacon' and 'liver and bacon', are collapsed into one. The first is a common formulaic expression used to mean 'keep out of trouble', while the second is a culture specific collocation, that is a case where two words are strongly associated (other examples include 'fish and chips' and 'bacon and eggs'). However, we need to move beyond the confines of the text itself in order to establish the identities of the addresser and addressee embedded in it; that is, who is the author of the note on the plate and who is it addressed to? Most people familiar with the cultural context would agree that the message has been written by a wife to her husband. It is his 'liver and bacon' which might be saved by 'a simple call'. The advertisement makes all sorts of assumptions, many of which are culture specific, for example that women are expected to cook their husbands' dinners but are not expected to wait at home beyond a certain time, either to serve the dinner or to keep it hot. There is also reference to particular sociocultural practices such as the keeping of family pets (some cultural groups do not treat domestic animals as family members in the way that many British families do).

In short, there are a number of discourses related to the institution of the family embedded in the text and, typically, these are not explicit. They are indicated by particular uses of language—ways of talking about such things as the nature of family meals and the keeping of pets. But the discourse relating to male and female roles in marriage was the one which some of my students failed to understand, the reason being that they came from cultures where wives would be available to serve hot food at whatever time suited the men of the family.

In fact, embedded in the advertisement are two major discourses in opposition to each other. The apparent assertiveness of the implied woman addressor, the author of the note, is undermined by the assumption that it is her responsibility to prepare hot dinners for her husband. In short, in spite of a superficial feminism, the prevailing discourse in the advertisement is undeniably sexist—wives are certainly expected to cook dinner even though they are not necessarily expected to be personally present to serve it, or to keep it hot in the oven beyond an agreed 'reasonable' time.

A definition of discourse which is related to social institutions such as marriage and the family provides us with an essentially social dimension to the consideration of both the activity of reading and written texts. In 3, 4, and 5 we shall look in more detail at firstly the social roles of readers, then the social context of reading, and finally the social meaning in texts.

3 Reading and social role

As readers we are frequently addressed in our social roles rather than our personal and individual ones. This is the case even in the kind of advertising which makes clever use of discourse to suggest that a product—for example a car or a perfume—has been designed 'just for you'. It is invariably a socio-economic group rather than an individual which is being addressed. And just as readers are addressed in their roles as parents, taxpayers, and, above all, as consumers, they also fulfil a whole range of social and professional roles through reading. Reading helps us not just to *do* but to *be*, that is, to act out certain behaviours associated with specific roles. For example, fathers in certain social groups read bedtime stories to their children; friends who live at some distance from one another maintain friendship through reading, and responding to, letters and greetings. To play an active role as a citizen one is usually required to understand public health warnings, respond to traffic signs, and fill in tax forms.

3.1 Reading communities

We can see then that reader roles are not only personal and private but are indicative of membership of the wider society, or a social grouping or community. Sociolinguists talk of *speech communities* (see, for example, Gumperz 1972). These are social groups which share both a language or language variety and conventions regarding its use. This means, for instance, that within the broader English speaking community there are sub-groups whose membership depends on class, national and ethnic identity, political affiliation, and so on. If we take a sociolinguistic view of reading, we can in the same way talk of communities of readers, or indeed of writers. Frank Smith coined the term the 'literacy club' (Smith 1983) to describe the group of people for whom reading and writing is a taken-for-granted daily event. Smith noted, moreover, that this club seems to deny entry to children from some social groups. We might want to add (see Wallace 1988) that there is not just a single club of readers but rather many clubs, and that as individuals we belong to a number of these, depending on our various social identities.

Even when reading on his or her own, there is a sense in which the reader remains a member of, for example, the community of sports page readers, readers of romantic fiction, or readers of feminist poetry. The kinds of reading options we take up say something about our membership of communities as well as individual preference.

We tend to bring to bear our assumptions and expectations about reading behaviour as we categorize people in terms of class, education, and age. So it is always interesting to try and match readers and text, and even more interesting when our predictions are disconfirmed. The conventionally dressed elderly woman on the train from Glasgow to Edinburgh was not reading Jane Austen or Agatha Christie as I had surmised but a modern classic about a rebellious teenager, J. D. Salinger's *Catcher in the Rye*, a book thought controversial enough to be banned in some schools in the United States.

► TASK 11

Think again about the kind of material you have read during the day. In what ways does this identify you as belonging to certain communities of readers? (Examples might be: request for tax (taxpayer); school report (parent); publisher's catalogue (EFL teacher).

3.2 Literacy events

Just as what being a reader means will vary from one society or cultural group to another, so will childrens' socialization into literacy. In a classic study, Shirley Brice-Heath (1983) talks of how different socio-economic communities take part in different kinds of what she calls 'literacy events'. She describes the uses of literacy sanctioned and supported by two communities which she calls Trackton and Roadville. Both are working class, but the first is black and the second white. Children in each community are socialized into literacy through the kinds of literacy events which are characteristic of their daily lives. Trackton children might, for instance, use their ability to read to help the postman in mail delivery, to recognize brand names when shopping, and to distinguish one television channel from another. There is no conscious creation of reading and writing tasks by the adults in the community. Children are left to find their own reading and writing tasks. Moreover, for this community reading is largely a public affair. Indeed the whole idea of reading silently and alone for pleasure may be a culturally alien one for many groups—a point that warrants consideration when attempting to devise a pedagogy to promote extensive reading in a second or foreign language.

► TASK 12

Which of the literacy events described here are familiar to you?

1 An adult is reading a story-book to a four-year-old. A younger child, aged two, joins the group but leaves to resume other activities as soon as the book is closed.

2 The mother of Henry, aged three, is showing him large cards on which words like 'nose', 'mouth', and 'mother' are written. She asks him to repeat the words.

3 Two friends sit at breakfast. One is reading a newspaper. At a certain point he opens discussion with his friend about the particular article he is reading.

4 A group of women are reading magazines in which there are horoscopes. Each reads out to the others her own horoscope.

These literacy events are influenced by the social roles sanctioned by the particular social groups to which the participants belong. Not all children will have books read to them at home by adults, for instance. Brice-Heath (1983) notes that children's early experiences of literacy may be in conflict with those of the school and classroom community. Indeed children whose literacy experiences are at odds with those sanctioned by the school may be simply classified by teachers as 'pre-' or 'non-literate'. However, Brice-Heath claims that all children who are growing up in literate communities will acquire, without specific instruction, some understanding of both the nature of print and of reading and writing behaviour.

3.3 Literacy or literacies?

If literacy development is, as the work of Brice-Heath indicates, strongly influenced by sociocultural environment, the question then arises as to whether literacy experiences may be so diverse that one should talk not of literacy as a single entity but of distinct 'literacies'. Street (1984), for instance, talks of different literacies among the groups he studied in Iran: he found that specific literacies developed in community or religious contexts and the kinds of cognitive and social abilities associated with them appeared to have little in common with school literacy. The example he gives is of 'Maktab' literacy, which is primarily knowledge of the Koran, acquired in Koranic schools known as Maktabs. This involves being able to recite relevant sections of religious texts without necessarily having even decoding ability, let alone the ability to read for meaning.

Does this mean that reading abilities cannot be generalized across literacy events? This is crucial when we consider readers from different languages and cultures. There are at least two issues to consider. First, the social contexts of a reader's first language literacy use may be very remote from those of second or foreign language literacy use in the classroom. Classrooms are themselves communities with their own uses of literacy and ascribed roles for teachers and learners, and there may be certain pedagogic practices, carried out in the name of reading or writing a second or foreign language, which are culturally alien to some learners. Second, of course, the languages themselves may be so different in the way they represent meaning in their written form that there is, arguably, no generalization from the first to the target language. Let us take each point in turn.

First, the concept of different context-dependent literacies is helpful in reminding us that, just as with spoken language, we may have a repertoire of literacies. And different communities, as well as different individuals within them, are likely to have 'strong' and 'weak' literacies. For instance, in my own case, examples of weak literacies would be the reading of computer manuals, train timetables, and signs in supermarkets.

▶ TASK 13

Do you feel that you personally have strong and weak literacies?

If so what reasons would you give for this? (These might include such things as upbringing, academic training, lifestyle, and personal traits and preferences.)

Many of us probably continue to feel inadequate when faced with texts such as income tax forms because of a general hostility to bureaucracy. A resistance to particular literacy events and the social events of which they are part, for example map reading, shopping, and form filling, may mean that we never become proficient in that particular literacy. Equally, a resistance to schooling may mean that the kinds of literacy promoted and valued by schooling are poorly developed, even though our repertoire of literacies may be quite adequate to the demands of other, non-academic contexts.

In short, we get to be good at reading, as with other abilities, firstly by means of practice, and secondly, as a result of the ways in which they are validated by our immediate community and society in general. We then need to ask how far skill in one kind of literacy is generalizable to other contexts. Both Brice-Heath (1983) and Street (1984) concede that it may be. Brice-Heath, for instance, argues that schools can effectively build on the kind of awareness of print which children have already acquired from family and community contexts. Equally, teachers of English as a second or foreign language can acknowledge diverse uses of literacy by inviting comment on their learners' first language literacy experiences.

If we turn to consider the ways in which different writing systems convey meaning, it has been argued, for example by Goodman (1984) that, while the contexts and functions of written language vary, reading as a *process* is unitary.

Reading is a unitary process both because it cannot be adequately broken down into separate skills (see **6.2** for a fuller discussion) and because we draw on similar processing strategies in the reading of all languages, even where the writing systems are very different. Buck (1979), for example, argues that the process of deriving meaning from written or printed symbols is similar across languages and across contexts. And Cummins and Swain (1986) talk of a Common Underlying Proficiency in language development whereby literacy skill is generalizable from the first to a second language.

It goes without saying that readers are likely to need more help and guidance in unfamiliar contexts. All of us have varying degrees of functional illiteracy. Educators, whether in first or second language situations, need to maximize learners' potential by drawing on existing strengths in either the first or other languages. In the case of second language readers, this means discovering what their repertoire of existing literacies is and what communities of readers they belong to. It also means attending to the contexts in which texts are encountered, which I turn to next.

4 Reading and social context

My use of the term 'discourse' in **2** can be related to three levels of context in the interpretation of any text—the immediate, the institutional, and the wider social context. These levels are similar to what Fairclough (1989) calls 'levels of social organisation': the level of the immediate social environment in which the discourse occurs; the level of the social institution which supports and legitimizes the selection of particular discourses, and the level of society as a whole.

It was argued, until quite recently, that a central feature of the written medium was its *lack* of dependence on context. Olson (1977), for instance, claims that written language is decontextualized and autonomous. This is, he says, an essential difference between spoken and written language. Admittedly Olson is talking of a particular kind of written language, what he calls 'essay' type literacy, rather than considering the whole range of written material as we are doing in this book, and it is true that the very restricted type of text which Olson deals with tends to rely less on contextual information than other types. Nonetheless, all forms of written language are both produced and received in a context which affects the way they are likely to be interpreted. As Fairclough (1989:151) says: 'interpreters (of texts) operate from the start with assumptions (which are open to later modification) about the contexts which influence the way in which linguistic features of a text are themselves processed, so that a text is always interpreted with some context in mind.' Let us begin with the immediate context of situation (that is, the physical and social environment in which the reading of a text takes place) before moving on to widen our sense of context by drawing on institutional and broader societal factors.

4.1 The immediate context of situation

We are surrounded by written texts. For example, we encounter them in the street, on public transport, and in the supermarket in the form of street signs, hoardings, and advertisements. These are examples of what we have called 'environmental print' (see **1.3**). With this kind of text, we are particularly dependent on information about the immediate physical context in which the message is embedded.

▶ TASK 14

Consider these items of print presented out of context. Is it possible to reconstruct a situational context for them?

old fashioned Italian slush . . . 1 502 BM . . . dinosaur tracks

Now if we embed them in the environments in which they originally occurred, you will probably agree that they are more readily interpretable.

We can widen our understanding of context of situation to include not just the circumstances in which we read a text but the factors which played a part in its production. As Nystrand puts it:

'even before I open my mail I know something about it. Once the envelope is open, my expectations are progressively set and fine-tuned by such details as logos, letterheads, type-face and mode of production (handwritten, typed, or dittoed) . . . these many layers of context which envelop the text provide important clues to the text's meaning.'
(*Nystrand 1986:56*)

Moreover, factors such as other participants in the literacy event—whether, for instance, a child is reading to a parent at home or a teacher at school—may affect the response to a particular text.

In short, reading involves not merely the interpretation of a text in its physical environment but the interpretation of the whole situation in which we encounter it. Even variables such as time of day, or year, may be crucial. Our reading of texts is closely tied not only to social convention, personal habit, passing mood or fancy, and immediate purpose, but may also be linked to factors such as time and place.

▶ ## TASK 15

Consider the likely circumstances of individual purpose, time, and place in the reading of the following texts:

text	*who?*	*where?*	*when?*	*why?*
weather forecast	driver	at home	start of	decide
information on voting			journey	on route
census form				
stock market report				
menu				
recipe				
horoscope				

Arguably, the ephemeral nature of some of the texts mentioned in Task 15 may make them unsuitable for foreign language classrooms, especially when a considerable time or distance separates writer and readers. However, it can also be argued that language learners have perfectly legitimate purposes, quite different from those of the original intended reader's, in reading such texts. The context, in this case the context of a language classroom, can create its own reading purposes. This is a point which is developed in Section Two of this book.

If we accept the notion of classrooms as communities (see **3.3**), it can be argued that teachers and learners create their own contexts along with certain roles and goals. Those of us who have visited different kinds of classroom will agree how powerfully the physical environment alone of a classroom conveys implicit as well as explicit messages. The presence of written material in whatever languages makes certain statements about how reading and other language activities are perceived and also about the norms and values of the classroom community. In other words, classrooms create their own expectations and value systems. These are partly determined by the norms and values of social institutions, such as schools (the institutional context), the nature of which is influenced by the behavioural norms and attitudes of the wider society (the social context). Let us look at the institutional context first.

4.2 The institutional context

Beyond the immediate context of situation in which any text is encountered, lies an institutional context. The existence of particular notices, signs, and documents demonstrates the power (both economic and social) of institutions such as the advertising media or the government. For example, both the style and content of public advertisements tell us a great deal about norms of behaviour, the bounds of what is felt to be public decency, and so on. Our knowledge of a society's key institutions helps us to anticipate when and where we might be likely to come across particular printed messages.

▶ TASK 16

Where might you expect to find these messages, which take the form of large-format computer printouts and are attached to the wall of the same room?

FOLLOW YOUR HEART AND YOUR DREAMS WILL COME TRUE
THE SMARTEST PERSON IN THIS ROOM IS YOU

One group of students from the Soviet Union suggested that these messages might be found in a psychiatrist's office. A group of British students made a similar guess. In fact I came across them in a primary classroom on the largest Navajo reservation in the United States. To me they communicated firstly an abounding optimism—dreams *can* come true—and secondly a highly individualistic and competitive ethic in which the achievement of the individual is seen as more important than any collective achievement of the group.

▶ TASK 17

Note all the written messages, for example warnings, instructions, and information, on the walls in your own classroom, staff-room, or common-room. What do these indicate about the institutional context?

The notices in schools and classrooms tell us about the nature of schooling as an institution in a particular society. In other words, what goes on in the immediate classroom context reflects certain institutional norms and values, not just of a specific school but of the institution of schooling in the wider society in which it exists.

4.3 The wider social context

Behind a particular text in its immediate and institutional contexts lies a complex set of values, beliefs, knowledge, and expected behaviours which are part of the shared culture of its author, or authors, and its intended reader. The two texts quoted above from the primary classroom on a Navajo reservation arguably reflect the values of the wider North American society rather than those of the immediate Navajo community. In the latter, individual achievement is, traditionally, less valued than in the former.

I was recently living in an English-speaking environment which is in some ways culturally quite different from the urban British environment I am familiar with. For instance, I had some initial difficulty with the discourse in the sign in Task 18.

▶   TASK 18

Can you predict the likely immediate and institutional context for this particular message?

The message above was 'marked' for me; that is, it stood out as odd rather than being unexceptional as it would be to most natives of the area. I came across it in the downtown area of a relatively small south-western American town. As well as knowledge of the immediate context, which in this case would mean knowing that the sign was placed in a central area of town, and knowledge of the institutional context, i.e. that local councils (signalled here as T.C.C.—Tucson City Council) are empowered to put up such signs, we might agree that still further kinds of knowledge will help us interpret the message. Here I should like to follow the framework provided by Anderson and Lynch (1987), in *Listening* in this Scheme, and classify the sources of information potentially available to us in the following way:

General factual knowledge: Guns are dangerous.
Local factual knowledge: The carrying of guns is not illegal.

and, of importance to our present discussion:

Sociocultural knowledge: It is not considered unusual for people to carry guns.
It is not considered, by many, undesirable for people to carry guns.

However, even when I am in possession of the relevant factual and socio-cultural knowledge, the text will continue to mean something different to me than to readers socialized in a different way. The carrying of guns will have a different value for me, much as has the flying of the Stars and Stripes in American front gardens on Thanksgiving Day. That is, even though I know *about* the sociocultural attitudes associated with the carrying of guns or displaying the American flag, the impact of the images representing these will be different.

We have been looking so far at minimal texts such as advertisements, and simple notices in their physical and social contexts, and the way the reader needs to draw on different levels of contextual knowledge in order to interpret them. Much longer texts also carry a whole set of cultural assumptions, and, to a greater degree than the texts we have so far considered, require interpreting. In 5 I shall consider ways of looking at these longer stretches of language.

5 Reading and social meaning

In 3 and 4 we looked at the social nature of reading in terms of the reader's role in any reading activity and the context in which the text is interpreted. Here we will explore in more detail the kinds of social meanings within texts and the kinds of resources available to readers for gaining access to these meanings. In doing so we will introduce two new concepts which share the fact that they are both socially constructed, *genre* and *schema*.

5.1 Genre

Traditionally genre was a term used in the description of literary forms such as 'ballad', 'novel', and 'epic poem'. It was then, for example by Aston (1979), extended as a concept to include other types of text, for example 'menu' or 'shopping list'. Still more recently the concept has been further extended to include the whole range of culturally recognizable types of language activity, both spoken and written. For example 'tutorial', 'medical examination', 'joke', 'essay', and 'thesis' can all be described as genres. Some genres will be exclusive to particular cultural or subcultural groups; others, such as jokes, will be cross-cultural but have different distinguishing features according to their cultural context.

Genres as social events

The most recent, and broadest, definition of genre brings it close to the well-established notion of *register*, described by Halliday (for example, 1978) as the characteristic lexis and structures used in talking about particular topics. For instance one can talk of 'journalese' or 'advertising' as a register. Martin, Christie, and Rothery (1987:59) however, claim that 'genre theory differs from register theory in the amount of emphasis it places on social purpose as determining variables in language use'. Swales (1990:53) similarly emphasizes the socially-determined nature of genres, describing them as 'communicative events which are socioculturally recognizable'. Genres are social events not only in terms of the social roles and purposes of those who create them as speakers or writers but because the communicative function of the resulting spoken or written text is recognizable to a particular community of listeners or readers. Swales (1990), alluding to different written responses to a job application, notes, for example, how there are culturally recognizable signals as to what is a 'good news' or a 'bad news' letter. In the former the news is conveyed early while the rest of the letter elaborates and clarifies. An enthusiastic response is assumed. In the latter, the news is presented after a preamble which 'prepares the ground' and the assumption tends to be that there will be no further communication. In short, the two kinds of letter are of different genres, argues Swales, because they have different organizational and grammatical features in keeping with their different communicative functions. Conversely, a sharedness of function will be a major defining criterion in establishing a shared genre.

Even when we are presented with short fragments of texts without any supporting contextual information it is frequently a genre-like label which first comes to mind while we are trying to identify them.

▶ TASK 19

How readily can you identify a genre for these text extracts?

1 The woman was lying dead on the floor when he came in. She was already dead and covered up from head to toe.

2 A mystery blonde may hold the key to a grim motorway murder in which a man was burned alive in a stolen car.

3 Notwithstanding previous requests, the lessees of nos 7 and 8 are the only two that have paid their contributions towards the removal of the asbestos from the obsolete boiler.

4 Eleven million people have said yes.

We are able to assign a genre label to each text extract firstly through our awareness of the kind of job it is doing. For example, is it informing, persuading, or requesting? We are aided by our experience of ways in which overall communicative function is conventionally conveyed through the use of formal and semantic features in different kinds of texts. For example, extract 1 is recognizable as the genre 'detective fiction' as it typically brings us into the middle of the action with the use of the definite article in 'The woman'. In contrast, extract 2 is from a newspaper report: characteristically of this genre, an indefinite article introduces new information with the opening noun phrase 'A mystery blonde'. Extract 3 contains the agentless subject typical of officialese; in other words we are not to be told from whom the request comes. In extract 4 it is the number of people mentioned which identifies the genre as some kind of advertisement: we would respond very differently to a text which read 'Two people have said yes'.

Genre and discourse
Genres are not only typified by communicative function, organizational features, syntax and lexis, and the social circumstances in which they arise. There are also powerful expectations about the kinds of discourses to be found in particular genres. The notions of genre and discourse as defined here are closely related in the sense that both carry socially-

determined meanings. 'Discourse carries meanings about the nature of the institution from which it derives; genre carries meaning about the conventional social occasions on which texts arise' (Kress 1985:20). We recognize both genre and discourse by virtue of being members of particular sociocultural groups, that is our social circumstances dictate both the genres and discourses we have access to. For instance, I do not have ready access to the genre of written legal documents, not only because of the difficulty created by particular formal features of such texts but because the conventional ways in which the law is written about—legal discourses—are unfamiliar to me.

In other words, particular discourses are characteristic of particular genres. This is not to say that there is a one-to-one relationship between genre and discourse: medical discourse, for instance, may be realized in different genres such as 'medical report', 'doctor–patient consultation', and so on. Nonetheless, genre and discourse interact in the sense that knowledge of the genre allows us to predict the likely occurrence of certain discourses: conversely, given particular discourses or discourse features we can frequently identify the genre. For instance in Extract 4 in Task 19 the use of a particular kind of culturally recognizable language allowed us to identify the text as an advertisement of some kind. And, in Task 9, for those of us familiar with the xenophobic discourse of certain popular British newspapers, the genre is once again readily identifiable from the text extract given.

▶ **TASK 20**

What genre is suggested by the discourse in the opening section of this text?

Once upon a time, in the village of Nsukka in Nigeria, there lived a beautiful young girl called Ndidi. Ndidi was the only child of her parents and so she was particularly precious to them.

   Now the house in which they lived was close to the forest. Her parents never allowed her to go out on her own because they knew there were many dangers in the forest.
(*Mellor, Raleigh, and Ashton 1984:12*)

Most of us can immediately identify the genre as 'folk tale', largely by means of the formulaic opening. In addition, we can draw on knowledge not only of the genre's typical vocabulary and structure but also of such things as ways of talking about how girls should behave (or, by implication, not behave) and the risks to which young girls are exposed. All these features belong to folk-tale discourse. So 'there were many dangers in the forest' is as much a feature of this discourse as words like 'beautiful', 'young', and 'precious', and as typical of folk tales as their narrative structure and outcomes. Above all, it is the function of the genre which determines what kinds of discourse are drawn upon by the writer. The moralizing nature of the genre would be lost, and the genre therefore cease to be socioculturally recognizable as a 'story with a moral', in the absence of discourses related to danger and disobedience. (Predictably, later on in the story, Ndidi disobeys her parents.)

5.2 Schemas

One way of accounting for our ability to recognize the source of the text in Task 20 is to argue that we have a *schema* for the folk-tale genre and its typical discourses. Schemas, or schemata as they are sometimes known, have been described as 'cognitive constructs which allow for the organization of information in long-term memory' (Widdowson 1983:34). Cook (1989:69) puts it thus: 'The mind, stimulated by key words or phrases in the text or by the context, activates a knowledge schema.' Widdowson and Cook are emphasizing the cognitive characteristics of schemas which allow us to relate incoming information to already known information. This covers the whole range of knowledge of the world, from everyday matters such as the fact that rain is wet or snow is white or guns can kill, to very specialized knowledge about nuclear physics or applied linguistics.

As well as allowing us to organize knowledge economically, schemas also allow us to predict the continuation of both spoken and written discourse. The first part of a text activates a schema, that is, calls up a schema which is either confirmed or disconfirmed by what follows. We may either call up the wrong schema altogether or need to keep readjusting it as the discourse in the text unfolds.

▶ **TASK 21**

What schema is called up by the opening lines of this novel? In what ways do you readjust your initial schema as you progress through the text?

Barrabas came to us by sea, the child Clara wrote in her delicate calligraphy.

Typically of a novel genre, we are invited to conjecture about Barrabas: Is the connection with the sea a crucial one? Is the biblical reference relevant? Is Barrabas a sailor of some kind—a pirate perhaps? Is he some kind of aquatic animal? We are not to be told immediately. The next we hear of Barrabas is seven lines later:

'Barrabas arrived on a Holy Thursday. He was in a despicable cage, caked with his own excrement and urine, and had the lost look of a hapless, utterly defenseless prisoner; but the regal carriage of his head and the size of his frame bespoke the legendary giant he would become.'
(Isabel Allende: *House of the Spirits*)

We are now likely to adjust our schema in the light of this further information. Barrabas is almost certainly an animal. But we still need to work out the relevance of much of the information provided. If the sea is not significant, is his arrival on Holy Thursday? In fact it is not until page thirty that we discover that Barrabas is a puppy!

Genre Schemas

We are able to tolerate uncertainty in the Barrabas text because we are familiar with the rules of the genre—in other words, we have a schema for the genre. Cook (1989) notes how in some genres such as 'joke' and 'literature' the device is frequently used of overturning the schema which the writer assumes will be called up by his or her discourse. Convention requires other genres to be more predictable. For instance, in the case of Task 20, as soon as we read 'once upon a time' and 'beautiful young girl', and 'dangers in the forest' we can very readily predict an outcome to the story.

Genre is frequently the category which is first called up when we are confronted with a text or fragment of text. The first question we tend to ask of any text is 'What kind of text is this?' This, as argued in 5.1, relates closely to our awareness of *why* the text has been written—that is, its communicative function. Thus, the initial response to the question 'What can you say about this text?' is likely to be 'novel' or 'newspaper report' or 'thriller'. My students, despite their difficulty in interpreting the 'dinner in the dog' text, were nonetheless all able to say that it was an advertisement. Of course, some genres are more recognizable than others and some, such as folk and fairy tales, arguably have universal discourses which relate less to specific social institutions than to universally experienced phenomena such as loss and recovery, or parting and reconciliation. It is for this reason that readers from a whole range of cultural backgrounds can fairly readily predict, for example, that Ndidi will indeed meet danger in the forest and that there will be a temporary parting from her parents with reconciliation as the resolution.

Topic schemas

If the first question we ask when confronted with a text is 'What kind of text is this?' the second tends to be 'What is the text about?' Our schematic knowledge may be organized round topics such as 'American football' or 'sociolinguistics'. We relate lexical items from the text to our schematic framework, so that for instance, most of us would identify 'programme—economy—inflation—policy' as part of a political discourse rather than a legal or theatrical one.

▶ ## TASK 22

Consider what kinds of topic knowledge are required to make sense of this text:

Leading industrials recorded a majority of falls in the 2p to 8p range. Gilts also kept a low profile, with conventionals down a quarter and index-linked three-eighths lower. Quiet builders provided a firm spot in Ward Holdings, up 17p to 177p following a 63 per cent upsurge in pre-tax profits. Golds relinquished 50 cents to a dollar.

Here the reader is less dependent on knowledge of the genre ('newspaper report') than knowledge of the topic—simply what is being talked about. Without access to very specialized kinds of knowledge of finance and business, the uninitiated reader will have some difficulty in relating lexical items such as 'falls', 'gilts', and 'builders' to construct a coherent text. However, the reader would have been helped by simply being given the general topic, thus being directed towards an appropriate schema. Just as a genre category such as 'fable' will help call up a schema so will, in this case, a topic one such as 'stock market'. The relevant lexis can then be accommodated to the appropriate schema. We can see how useful the provision of a title or heading is in allowing the reader to access schematic knowledge. Book titles, newspaper headlines, and advertising copy clearly serve this purpose.

▶ **TASK 23**

What schemas, either of genre or topic, or both, are called up by these headings?
1 Stay of Execution for Hostage
2 The Sly Fox and the Little Red Hen
3 The Skull Beneath the Skin
4 Even Softer Facial Tissue

In 2, for example, the introduction of the two animals with typical epithets is likely to trigger a schema for 'fable', while in 4 the use of the comparative form unlinked to a following noun phrase (softer than what?) signals an advertisement. In 3 the word 'skull' suggests that the topic is death, while the use of the definite article rather than naming a human possessor is typical of the title of a murder story. In 1, the absence of an article before 'stay' and 'hostage' along with the lexis 'execution' and 'hostage' clearly indicate both the genre ('newspaper headline') and topic (the delayed sentence of death on someone who has been kidnapped, probably by a terrorist group).

The sociocultural nature of schemas
Schema theorists, as Swales (1990) notes, have been mostly concerned with cognitive aspects of text processing. But schematic knowledge also has sociocultural aspects. Admittedly some knowledge is universal. We can assume, for instance, that there will be generally shared schemas

about the nature of rain, snow, and guns. However we are soon likely to find ourselves up against cultural and subcultural differences. We have already noted, for instance, that the discourses relating to the possession of guns may be different between communities in the United States and Britain. This is largely because, although there is likely to be shared knowledge about the appearance and uses of guns, there will be different attitudes to them. This difference of attitude is crucial. In the case of guns it may relate to attitudes to circumstances in which they should be used or carried, which in turn relate to more deep-seated attitudes to do with notions of freedom and control (i.e. the personal freedom to carry a gun versus the need to control individual behaviour). Thus schemas are not just cognitive constructs to do with the mental organization of concepts but also social–psychological constructs which allow us to attach particular values and attitudes to that knowledge. They are shaped by the sorts of social experiences which readers bring to texts.

Someone reading in a second language may encounter difficulty when confronted with highly culture-specific content. First, some genres and topics are themselves culture specific—examples include 'limerick' and 'cricket'. Second, different groups may interpret the same texts differently because they bring different schemas to bear on them. In an often-quoted study by Steffenson, Joag-Dev, and Anderson (1979), two groups of adult students, white North Americans and Indians respectively, were asked to read and recall two letters describing a typical American and a typical Indian wedding. There were clear cross-cultural differences in the way information was recalled and interpreted.

There may also be difficulty caused not so much by overall topic or genre but by particular, frequently idiomatic, phrases in the text which are liable to call up divergent schemas. For instance my Soviet students missed the culinary reference in 'save your liver and bacon' in Task 10— they read this as 'save your liver', thereby calling up a medical schema. Other more local misunderstandings may be caused by the introduction into a text of particular phenomena, events, persons, and places. And, as noted in **2.2**, along with knowledge of what or who these are we need knowledge of the discourses which typically accompany them. For instance, in Britain, there are typical ways of writing about women politicians in the popular press or the Royal Family in women's magazines. A British person may need only a very brief snatch of discourse from this type of text to call up the relevant genre schema. However, someone from another culture may have more problems with 'firebrand Benazir Bhutto' or 'Di, devoted mum', both typical examples respectively of the language of the popular press and womens' magazines where a restricted range of adjectives is used to describe women (see Andersen (1988) for a description of these characteristic discourses).

Moreover, some discourses are ephemeral, alluding to phenomena which hit the news and then fade, for example those related to fashion, health scares, and scandals. This means that we frequently need to readjust our conventional schemas, especially when confronted with genres, such as newspaper reports and articles, whose content is essentially ephemeral.

To conclude, the reader needs to bring together linguistic knowledge, for example knowledge of how texts are constructed, and familiarity with the discourses within a text, to draw upon a relevant schema. This can create difficulty where the discourses in a text relate to highly ephemeral and culture-specific phenomena, as in Task 24.

▶ ## TASK 24

What kind of schematic knowledge of genre and topic, and their associated discourses, is the reader required to draw on in this text?

Clanger-o-gram

Kissogram girl Alison Johnson boobed when she was hired to surprise public-school housemaster John Wood. For Alison, 38-24-36, dashed into astonished headmaster, John Rees's study—and kissed him by mistake. She had to wait for more than an hour, wearing only a skimpy basque and suspenders, before she tracked down Mr Wood in the dining hall. Hundreds of boys cheered as she finally planted a smacker on the right man.

A textual analysis here would allow us to see that the second sentence beginning with 'For' explains the first—we might thus, if we did not know it, be able to work out a meaning for the word 'boobed', especially if we related it to the phrase 'by mistake'. Equally 'the right man' can be identified as 'Mr Wood' on the principle of pronoun reference. However, in order to appreciate the text more fully, we need to be familiar with the discourses typical of this highly culture-specific genre which we might identify as 'report, intended to be humorous, in a popular newspaper'. An example of such discourse might be the giving of the woman's body measurements. We also need to draw on a schema for the topic 'sending kissograms' and for the other phenomena mentioned in the text, such as 'public-school housemaster'. Moreover part of our schematic knowledge is knowledge not just of what kissogram girls and public schoolboys *are*, but of *why* they might behave in particular ways in particular situations, related to more general knowledge of ways of behaving in the target culture. Why for instance did the boys cheer as 'she finally planted a smacker on the right man'? Is this:

– something that always follows the succesful outcome of a kissogram?
– the conventional response to a joke of whatever kind?
– the way public schoolboys and other all-male groups often behave?

Moreover, as noted above, it is not just a question of interpreting the description of facts, phenomena, or behaviour but of being aware of a range of different attitudes to them, even if we do not personally share those attitudes. An example from this text might be that in Britain it is culturally acceptable in certain contexts for half-naked women to kiss strange men.

I have argued in 5 that the kinds of meanings we gain from texts are largely socially determined in that we draw on our knowledge of the typical social occasions on which a genre is employed to serve particular social goals. Our schematic knowledge of the genre and the topic with which it deals, as well as more local and specific knowledge, allows us to reconstruct particular discourses from the text. Moreover, we are guided in our interpretations by our own purposes, social roles, and the context in which we encounter the text. It is these complex private purposes and interests along with social identities and experiences which influence our interaction with a text in the course of reading, as I discuss more fully in 6.

6 The reading process

My aim in **6** is to bring together the main strands of our previous discussion about the roles of reader, context, and text in order to present a view of reading which incorporates both social and individual perspectives. This view is dynamic rather than static—that is, it emphasizes a reader's progression through a text rather than the text itself. It means looking at reading as a process rather than as a product. As Alderson and Urquhart (1984) point out, a product view relates only to what the reader has 'got out of' the text while a process view investigates how the reader may arrive at a particular interpretation.

For some years now, researchers into both first and second language reading have argued against the view that texts are self-contained objects, the meaning of which it is the reader's job merely to recover. They have proposed a dynamic relationship between text and reader. Texts do not 'contain' meaning; rather they 'have potential for' meaning. This potential is realized only in the interaction between text and reader. That is, meaning is created in the course of reading as the reader draws both on existing linguistic and schematic knowledge and the input provided by the printed or written text.

6.1 Reading as a psycholinguistic process

Frank Smith (1971) was one of the first researchers to characterize reading as process by charting the reader's path through a text rather than making judgements of comprehension based on reading outcomes. He described reading as 'the reduction of uncertainty'. That is, as we progress through a text, our choices of what to select are constrained, often heavily, both by features within the text itself and those external to it, to do, for instance, with the kinds of schematic knowledge discussed in 5.

▶ TASK 25

Complete the following short texts. Consider what factors operate in the reduction of uncertainty to constrain your choices in completing them appropriately.

1 The phone . . .   4 Bush to meet . . .
2 He picked up the . . .   5 Fish and . . .
3 Chr . . .

Smith's own famous example, 'The captain ordered the mate to drop the an＿' leads to his discussing the reduction of uncertainty under four headings, namely 'graphic information', 'phonetic information', 'syntactic information', and 'semantic information'. For instance, as far as graphic information is concerned, our knowledge of English spelling tells us that there is a limited number of possibilities as to which letter might follow 'an＿'. 'P' for instance would not be a possibility as there are no English words which have the letter sequence a—n—p. Phonetic information also plays its part in reducing the possibilities as to what kinds of sounds can co-occur. Uncertainty is further reduced by our knowledge that, syntactically, only an adjective or noun phrase can follow the item 'the'. Finally, with regard to semantic information, our propositional knowledge restricts the kinds of things that it is humanly possible to drop—for example 'anticyclone' would not be a possibility here. We can also draw on more specific schematic knowledge to predict what kinds of things captains might reasonably ask mates to do. We need, in short, to call up a 'nautical' schema which will give us 'anchor' as the most likely item. It should be added, however, that genre knowledge will tend to override other knowledge sources, so, for instance, if we know that the genre is fairy story or fantasy, 'angry mermaid' might be a more likely option than 'anchor'!

Kenneth Goodman, in a famous article written in 1967, talks of reading as 'a psycholinguistic guessing game' in ways very similar to Smith. In Goodman's account, the reader makes use of three cue systems, represented by three levels of language within the text, which he terms graphophonic, syntactic, and semantic. In other words, first, readers make use of their knowledge of the visual and phonetic features of English discussed in **2.1**; second, they draw on knowledge of syntactic constraints such as possible kinds of word order in English and, third, they are aware of semantic constraints related to knowledge of the meaning of words and what kinds of words collocate with others. Moreover, semantic or propositional knowledge is mediated by schematic knowledge of the kind discussed in **5**. Syntactic and semantic cues are usually so powerful that effective readers only need to resort to the graphophonic level to refine and check their predictions. Frequently, even if a word is deleted altogether from a text, contextual support for the item is strong enough for it to be readily guessed or replaced by a near synonym.

▶ **TASK 26**

What syntactic and semantic cues are there in this text to provide help in filling the gaps?

The coffee came and with it a slice of ＿＿＿. Burden eyed it ＿＿＿. It was sometime since he had ＿＿＿ and there was a long ＿＿＿ ahead.

Knowledge of the syntactic possibilities of English will determine, for instance, that a noun phrase must follow 'of'. At the same time, awareness of semantic constraints allows us to predict a concrete noun rather than an abstract one like 'happiness'. This knowledge is refined by culture-specific knowledge of the kinds of things that might typically be consumed with coffee in a particular context at certain times of the day or night (examples might be 'bread', 'cake', or 'toast' rather than 'banana' or 'cheese'). Semantic cues can operate at sentence level, at paragraph level, or, more globally, in the wider text. For instance in the case of the text in Task 26, the preceding narrative has established that it is 8 o'clock in the evening. This makes 'cake' a likelier option than 'toast' to fill the first gap and 'night' more likely than 'day' to fill the last.

Goodman was interested not just in identifying cueing systems in reading but in the ways readers, in particular learner readers, miscued, that is read something other than the word on the page. Learner readers, in reading aloud, may miscue on any or all three levels of language identified as cueing systems in Goodman's 1967 article. That is the reader may read for 'He caught his small ball':

1 He *cough* his small ball. (graphophonic miscue)
2 He caught *the* small ball. (syntactic miscue)
3 He caught his *little* ball. (semantic miscue)

These examples are idealized and in fact most miscues show the influence of two or even three cueing systems. It is rarely the case, for instance, that a miscue is only graphophonic, that is that it focuses exclusively on the visual and phonetic features of the word without fitting the preceding syntax or making any sense at all.

Goodman's work focuses on miscues revealed to us through the reading-aloud process. More recently, other researchers have tried to capture what happens during the silent reading process. Cavalcanti (1987), for instance, asked her subjects to read silently but to 'think aloud' when they noticed a pause in their reading process which indicated a potential 'problem' situation, either because of their inability to process the text at that point or because of exceptional interest. In this way, Cavalcanti aimed to establish the location of the problem encountered, its nature, and the way it was dealt with.

Even in everyday—not research—contexts, we are frequently aware that we have encountered a particular problem in the course of silent reading: we may even be able to characterize it as a particular kind of miscue. For instance a graphophonic miscue would be indicated where we have mentally substituted a particular word with one which is very similar visually and phonetically, but does not fit the context. Admittedly, in the case of experienced readers, this happens rarely, for example when one is tired or preoccupied. I can recall, when in the United States, casually wondering why a message on a packet which confronted me on opening the refrigerator should read 'absorbs refrigerator doors'. A quick double take showed that in fact it read 'absorbs refrigerator odors' (clearly unfamiliarity with American spelling played a part here).

6.2 Reading as a unitary and selective process

The main principle of Smith's and Goodman's approach is that reading is a unitary process (see **3.3**). One premise of this view is that it is not possible to identify specific skills which can be built up in any hierarchical way to produce an effective reader. In this, they are supported by the research of Lunzer and Gardner (1979) who carried out a detailed study of secondary school children reading in their first language. Lunzer and Gardner found that there was no correlation between generally effective reading and performance on a supposed hierarchy of different subskills such as using phonetic analysis or perceiving a sequence of ideas. In fact they were unable to identify a hierarchy of skills as such. What chiefly characterized effective readers was an ability and willingness to reflect on what they were reading. In short, after the administration of a detailed series of tests, Lunzer and Gardner concluded that reading comprehension was best described as a 'unitary aptitude', a conclusion consistent with Smith's and Goodman's approach.

This unitary view of the reading process has led researchers to talk of reading *strategies* rather than distinct *skills*. Effective readers draw selectively on a range of strategies, described more fully in **7**, which are determined by reader purpose, text-type, and context. Efficient readers predict and sample, selecting the minimal visual information consistent with their prediction. They do not need to use all the cues. As Goodman (1987) puts it, they 'tune out irrelevant information' or what we might call visual 'noise' just as effective listeners tune out verbal 'noise'. It is this selectivity, along with the ability and willingness to reflect which I have already mentioned, which is the key to effective reading.

While Smith's and Goodman's approach has been influential in the teaching of reading in both first and second languages, some second language reading researchers, especially in the United States, have felt that the approach neglects what they call 'bottom-up' processing, that is, attention to the specific graphophonic and syntactic features of texts. It focuses, they argue, overmuch on 'top-down' processing, that is, features related to schematic knowledge of genre and topic. Eskey (1988) for instance, claims that second language readers need to attend more to 'bottom-up' features than do first language readers. Eskey's view is based on the incontrovertible fact that the former will have weaker linguistic competence than the latter and will therefore have less ability to draw on the range of cues—both within and external to the text—which are available to readers in a first language. One response to this situation would be not to encourage different reader strategies for second language readers, but to ensure that text, context, and reading task give maximum support to the second language learner's current linguistic and schematic knowledge. Ways of doing this are suggested in Section Two.

6.3 Sociolinguistic factors in the reading process

What the psycholinguistic accounts of Smith and Goodman tended to neglect was the social nature of the reading process. Consequently, later descriptions of the reading process, including Goodman's more recent work, have turned to the consideration of sociolinguistic factors, that is the way language use, in this case written language use, is affected by factors both in the immediate communicative situation between reader and writer and in the wider institutional and sociocultural context discussed in **3**. For it is not just psychological, cognitive, or affective factors which influence our interpretation of texts, but social ones. Kress (1985:44) says 'so although from the individual's point of view her or his reading is "just my personal opinion", that personal opinion is socially constructed'. In other words, we are never just talking of an individual response. Fish (1980) argues similarly when he talks of readers as members of 'interpretative communities' echoing Smith's description of children's socialization into literacy as 'joining the literacy club' (see **3.1**).

One might argue that we are all members of a variety of different interpretative communities, that is we interpret texts in the light of schemas which are constructed through exposure to a range of genres and discourses encountered as members of a number of different social groups. We share ways of interpreting texts with those of a similar social class or ethnic group, or of similar religious and political beliefs. That our personal interpretations will never be identical with those of others is because we have multiple social identities, any of which may be salient in our reading of a particular text.

I have argued that in taking a process view of reading it is important to see it as involving not just psychological processes, but also social factors related to our membership of interpretative communities. We now need to consider more closely the ways in which these factors are involved in the particular interaction between reader and writer.

6.4 The interaction between reader and writer

We have seen that writers take for granted that their readers are in possession of certain kinds of knowledge of the world. They make very broad assumptions about the kinds of things that will not be perceived as problematic by their readers. In other words, writers take for granted that readers will be able to call up particular schemas. Readers are also classified in more specific ways by mass producers of written material such as book publishers, and magazine and newspaper editors. Titles of publications often explicitly address specific readership groups, for example

Marxism Today, Woman, New Civil Engineer, or *EFL Gazette.* If you are not one of the group of intended readers, the effect when reading one of these publications is of eavesdropping on a dialogue between the writer and the writer's imagined or—to use the term I shall adopt in this book—*model reader.* Differing background knowledge and cultural assumptions may make it difficult to interpret texts in a way which corresponds with the writer's schema. Moreover, readers are not simply categorized as members of social groups but 'positioned', that is invited to concur with the beliefs and world view of the producer of the text, as indicated by the dominant discourses within it. As one of my students said about 'The blame that Spain must share'—'the writer wants us to think that he is not biased'.

As well as categorizing and positioning their readers, writers conduct an ongoing dialogue with them (Widdowson 1979). The assumption of shared political and social attitudes affects the nature of the dialogue in the sense that writers anticipate reader objection or agreement at particular points in their discourse. In other words, writers do not just imagine a particular kind of reader, they anticipate particular kinds of response to statements or claims they make in the course of constructing their texts. In the following extract from the introduction by Judith Stinton to *Racism and Sexism in Children's Books*, for instance, the writer responds to an imagined objection on the part of her model reader.

▶ TASK 27

1 What kind of response might the model reader make at the end of this text extract?

2 How do you think the writer might respond in turn to this imagined response?

'Black people are often anonymous figures in children's literature written by white authors. Timothy in 'The Cay' is lucky enough to be given a first name. None of the characters in 'Sounder' has a name at all (apart from the dog!). This is obviously a conscious literary device to bring universality to the story: even so it's an ill-chosen one.'
(*Stinton 1979:2*)

One might imagine a reader response to the effect 'But surely many stories do not give names to their characters?' or 'Are you saying that only black writers can describe the black experience?' In fact the writer resumes thus 'This doesn't mean, though, that white writers should never try to describe the black experience . . .'

There is also a temperamental factor in the interaction between writer and reader. Writers may reveal themselves as authoritarian or liberal, particularly in didactic genres. A dilemma for textbook writers, for instance, is how to sound suitably authoritative without sounding bossy. The writer who assumes too little background knowledge will sound patronizing; too much, and the charge is likely to be obscurity.

6.5 Submissive and resistant readers

How far can, or should, readers resist a writer's positioning? One case for submitting to it rests on the belief that, whether we agree or disagree with him or her, any debate as to the meaning of the text must finally be answered in favour of the writer as its producer. However, there are some difficulties in arguing that the 'real' meaning is 'what the author intends'. Almost certainly, for instance, the writer of 'The blame that Spain must share' would deny the intention or even the presence of racism in his discourse. He would be likely to argue that the 'real' meaning was a perfectly fair and proper attempt to set the record straight. And of course, many readers, those who are part of his model readership, would agree. But they do not therefore have exclusive rights to the ownership of the text's meaning, Arguably, an oppositional or subversive reading is as legitimate as one which is intended by the writer.

Scholes (1985) takes a more cautious view, arguing that initially we do need to submit to the writer's intended meaning as we find it evidenced in the text. Otherwise the danger is that we will project our own subjective modes of thought on to the text and fail to acknowledge the writer's position. However Scholes also stresses that in the reading of both literature and other texts the eventual goal must be critical reading. He puts it thus: 'In an age of manipulation, when our students are in dire need of critical strength to resist the continuing assaults of all the media, the worst thing we can do is to foster in them an attitude of reverence before texts' (1985:16). An over-reverential attitude may be a particular temptation for second language learners or cultural minority readers who find foreign language texts intimidating as a result of lack of linguistic or schematic knowledge.

Scholes implies that students of literature at least may need a fair degree of guidance in order to become critical readers. Widdowson (1984), on the other hand, suggests that readers are able to make their own choices as to what kind of stance to adopt towards a text, depending on their purposes in reading it. He also argues that their position will shift as their purpose shifts. Thus readers may choose to be 'submissive' or 'assertive'. The submissive reader's interpretation is likely to be the one intended by the writer, while the assertive reader, with distinct purposes of his or her own, can derive quite remote interpretations. Widdowson puts it thus: '[The reader] is free to take up whatever position suits his purpose on the dominance/dependence scale' (page 223).

► TASK 28

Think of two reading experiences which you have had recently, one in which you responded assertively and one in which you responded submissively.

1 What dictated your response in each situation? Consider your purpose, the type of text, and the situation in which you were reading it.

2 Did any problems arise in being either too submissive or too assertive?

If the reader is too submissive, Widdowson claims, he or she may accumulate information without accommodating it into the schematic structure of existing knowledge. If the reader is too assertive, 'he may distort the writer's intentions and deny access to new knowledge and experience' (page 226). We might want to add, though Widdowson does not suggest this, that we may, as readers, be generally disposed to be critical or acquiescent for temperamental reasons.

Widdowson allows readers a fair degree of autonomy in their response to texts. Others such as Kress (1985) have questioned how much choice readers have in the stance they take up in relation to a particular text or genre. That is, submissiveness is imposed and assertiveness is not an option for them. There are two major factors which might work against the personal freedom of the reader to accommodate the text to his or her individual purposes. First, some readers, for broadly social rather than personal reasons, may be in a weak position to resist particular discourses in particular genres. For instance children in school are not generally enabled or encouraged to assert themselves against the prevailing discourses in school texts. And, as I have argued above, second and foreign language learners may also, though for different reasons, feel reluctant to challenge the text. Here reading is still interactive but the interaction is an unequal one.

However, this should not be taken in too deterministic a spirit. Kress goes on to describe how the good reader is able to resist positioning by the text and reconstruct a reading position more congenial to him or her. Indeed a hallmark of good reading, he argues, is exactly this kind of resistance. At several points in this book I have invited my reader to read texts in a subversive way: I have, for instance, suggested resistance to what I see as institutionalized xenophobia revealed through the discourses about greedy uncooperative Spaniards (2.2). However, I am aware that my reader may choose to resist the positioning that I am undoubtedly exerting and will wish to read these texts in quite a different way.

A second point is that some genres and the discourses embedded in them are in themselves heavily constraining. Certainly genres differ in the amount of positioning they impose on the reader. Particular texts, as examples of genre types, differ strikingly in the amount of freedom they allow for alternative readings—alternative that is to the reading which is implicit in the dominant discourses within the text.

The semiotician Eco (1981) has talked of 'open' and 'closed' texts. Open texts allow their readers a wide range of interpretative choices while closed texts are those which demand conformity, encouraging only a restricted range of interpretations. In fact, one cannot talk simply of open and closed texts—rather there is a continuum of genres with legal texts being probably the most closed and poetry the most open. The more open the text the more opportunity there is for diverse interpretations.

So far in this discussion I have tended to favour the freedom of the reader over the authority of the writer. Does this mean that the reader can do what he or she will with the text? Is one interpretation as good as another? The answer is clearly 'no'. First, we need to remember that the text exerts its own constraints to do with the conventionally accepted meanings of the words which constitute it. If, for instance, the text reads 'Ndidi went into the wood' it would be perverse of a reader to claim that the meaning of 'wood' is 'house'. We necessarily, as with all modes of language, need to work within a shared formal and conceptual framework. Even when we move into more disputed territory, the interpretation of the communicative function of statements in the text (for example, *why* does the author tell us that 'Ndidi went into the wood'?), one interpretation is not as good as another. Some readers are in a stronger position than others to provide a well-informed interpretation because they have a greater experience of the genre and understanding of the circumstances in which the text was composed. Readers are also helped by an awareness of the ways in which a particular text relates to other texts within or across genres. This principle of textual cross-reference is known as *intertextuality*.

6.6 Intertextuality

The production and reception of a given text depends upon the writer's and reader's knowledge of other texts (see, for example, de Beaugrande and Dressler 1981). Texts have a history and may fit into a sequence of other texts. For instance, 'The blame that Spain must share' can be interpreted as one of a series of texts on the topic of lager louts to appear in the British press in the summer of 1989. As writers, like readers, are influenced by the dominant discourses of the time, it is helpful to know something about the circumstances in which a text was produced. It may also be helpful to know how a particular text relates to other texts by the same author and to other contemporary genres. All texts contain traces of other texts, and frequently they cannot be readily interpreted—or at least fully appreciated—without reference to other texts. Examples may range from the literary and specific, for example Eagleton's (1983:8–9) 'Some texts are born literary, some achieve literariness, and some have literariness thrust upon them' (clearly echoing Shakespeare's *Twelfth Night*) to broader influences from other genres. Fairclough (1989) notes how some genres, notably advertising, have colonized a whole range of discourses which are conventionally associated with other genres.

▶ TASK 29

What genre does this text belong to? On which other genre or genres has the writer of this text drawn. Why, do you think?

'Before the night was through they would reveal a lot more to each other than just their watches. Copacabana danced below as he came face to face with her bewildering elegance.

Her movements held him spellbound as she slipped her immaculately manicured fingers inside her leather handbag to emerge with a cigarette pack.'

This text is a pastiche of romantic fiction with its typical discourses centering around money, luxury goods, and exotic locations—what has been called a 'sex and shopping' genre. The producers of the text clearly want to flatter the model reader by assuming that he or she will identify with the life-style presented. However, the skilled reader will quickly recognize it as an advertisement, though it is not immediately clear whether it is for cigarettes, nail-varnish, a package holiday, or—as is in fact the case—for a type of watch.

Sometimes a genre is even more heavily disguised than the example in Task 29 in order to achieve a particular calculated effect. For example, what looks like a personal letter may in fact be a public appeal for money from a charity or political organization. Frequently the effect of this is to disguise the function of the communication, and therefore to conceal the 'real' genre.

▶ TASK 30

What are the 'real' genres of the three extracts below? What other genres have been used to disguise them? What are the reasons for these particular disguises?

☆

a christmas wish...

If undelivered return to: The Spastics Society, PO Box 39, Liverpool.

THE QUESTORS THEATRE

MATTOCK LANE, LONDON W5 5BQ
Telephones: 01-567 0011 (Admin.) 01-567 5184 (Box Office) 01-567 8736 (Membership)
PRESIDENT: SIR MICHAEL REDGRAVE CBE
VICE-PRESIDENTS: SIR BRIAN BATSFORD, JUDI DENCH OBE, ALFRED EMMET OBE
THEATRE MANAGER: JOHN GARFORTH

Dear Cathy

I expect you get an awful lot of junk mail through the
post, most of which you throw straight in the bin?   I
don't blame you.

However, I wonder whether, by mistake, you threw away
the letter I sent you last month reminding you that your
annual subscription to the Questors was due? Just in
case you did, I thought I'd write to you again because it
would be a shame if George, our new computer, thought you
meant to resign when you really were dying to renew for
another year. We've got a varied and interesting season
of plays and social events planned, which I'm sure you
wouldn't want to miss!

As a measure of my appreciation for your
support, I thought I'd enclose this photo. It
captures a moment during my 1987 'Long
March' – for a nuclear free Britain – from the
U.S. base at Faslane to the British nuclear
bomb factory at Burghfield. Here we are planting
a Cherry Tree outside Aldermaston on Hiroshima
Day.
            Many, many thanks for all your help
and support,

Bruce Kent

These texts are representative of the way in which mass mailings have
been personalized over recent years, presumably in an attempt to stop the
reader from immediately discarding the material. Indeed, extract 2 opens
by anticipating just such a response: 'I expect you get an awful lot of junk
mail . . . most of which you throw straight in the bin?'

In **6** we have seen how the reading process is interactive in several ways:
first, there is interaction between the levels of language within the text
which the reader draws on in the course of reading; then there is interaction between reader and writer, and, finally, texts themselves interact on
the principle of intertextuality.

6.7 Conclusion

If we see both writing and reading as social processes, many factors contribute to the construction of meaning in written texts. Examples include the social roles and experiences of writer and reader and their respective purposes, and also the context in which a text is produced and interpreted.

It is still, of course, on any single occasion the individual reader who is confronted with the individual text. Finally, it is not that personal opinion and judgement is unimportant, but that we need to locate the individual within a social context, to be aware of the whole range of sociocultural experiences and attitudes which act as the backdrop to any particular interpretation. In fact the typical reader has much richer resources than is sometimes supposed, and readers from diverse linguistic and cultural backgrounds may have particularly important contributions to make to the interpretation of texts. On occasion they may need to do harder interpretative work than readers from the same background as the writer, but this in itself can help them become more critical and reflective readers. Moreover, simply because as foreign or second language readers they are often not part of a text's model readership, they may be in a better situation to resist its positioning and to bring helpful, novel, and entirely valid interpretations to the text.

Demonstration
Teaching approaches and materials

In Section One of this book we looked at different ways of characterizing reading, as product and process, and as text and discourse. In particular the social interactive nature of the process was emphasized. In this section I shall look firstly, in **7**, at the implications of a process approach for the teaching of early reading, moving on, in **8**, to focus specifically on the learning context of second language readers. In **9** I shall look at the role of the text in the second language classroom, and in **10** at ways in which teachers can facilitate the interaction with texts through the use of particular kinds of tasks. Finally, in **11**, I shall consider some approaches which take account of the sociocultural nature of the reading process.

7 Early reading: teaching and learning

7.1 Getting started

It is possible to talk of product and process approaches not only in relation to mature reading but also in connection with the learning and teaching of early reading. A product approach to early reading tends to assume that there are specific behaviours which must be learned before instruction in 'reading proper' can commence. Students are judged to have begun to learn to read only when such instruction begins and, on commencement of instruction, progress is measured through achievement on specific tests and tasks. If, on the other hand, we view learning to read as a developmental process it is not at all easy to say at which point reading begins. Is it when a child turns the pages of a book and tells a story—which is not the story in the book? Is it when a child recognizes his or her own name in print? Is it even earlier, when he or she climbs on to an adult's knee to take part in the reading of a story to an older brother or sister?

7.2 Different views of the learning to read process

It can be interesting to ask children themselves what their views of the learning to read process are. Weaver (1980) quotes a study by Harste in which children were asked to give their views.

► TASK 31

What views of reading, and the process of learning to read, do these comments suggest?

'It's filling out workbooks.'
'Pronouncing the letters.'
'It's when you put sounds together.'
'Reading is learning hard words.'
'Reading is like think . . . you know, it's understanding the story.'
'It's when you find out things.'

The children were asked these questions in the context of school. They appear to indicate that learners gain an idea of what reading is from what teachers do and ask them to do in the name of reading, and from the nature of the materials they work with. While these were fairly young children learning to read in their first language, it is likely that comparable responses would be produced in many second and foreign language situations.

7.3 A skills approach to learning to read

Some of the comments in Task 31 suggest that learning to read is seen as building up particular skills. Indeed learning to read may be strongly associated just with one skill such as 'pronouncing the letters'. A skills approach to early reading tends to be characterized in terms of the ability to perform discrete tasks which do not necessarily involve the ability to make sense of a written message. The approach is essentially 'atomistic', as Cook (1989) describes it, in that, whether we are talking about reading or language education more generally, the data we are dealing with is divided up into supposedly manageable learning chunks. The teacher's role is that of an instructor who transmits items of knowledge, or who teaches or drills activities, rather than drawing on and extending the learners' existing knowledge and abilities. The emphasis tends to be exclusively on *what* is to be taught, rather than also considering *how* learning takes place. Early reading skills are exemplified by, for example, performance on certain kinds of motor skills, the ability to discriminate shapes and patterns, and phonic and word recognition skills. 'Phonics', as the method is popularly called (see **2.1**) involves the ability to match up letters (or 'graphemes') to some kind of sound representation. It tends to be assumed that phonic skill is displayed by the ability to read aloud with a 'good'—that is a native-like, standard English—pronunciation. Word recognition skills, often associated with the so-called 'look and say' method, involve the ability to name whole words, whether presented in a textual or situational context or not.

Materials for both first and second language learners may, either explicitly or implicitly, focus on one or several of these skills.

▶   TASK 32

In the extracts given on this and the next page what kinds of skills are being presented or practised?

Reading

Mrs. Rich always gets up early in the morning. She takes a shower and then has a big breakfast. She usually drinks two or three cups of coffee. After breakfast she drives to work.

She usually has a busy day at the office. She reads her mail, sees many business people, has meetings, and sometimes goes to the factory. She often eats lunch at the factory. After work
5   she comes home and cooks dinner. Mrs. Rich likes to cook and her son, Michael, just loves to eat.

She usually stays home in the evening, but sometimes she goes out with friends or with her family.

Mrs. Rich takes a bath every night before she goes to bed. She loves to read the newspaper
10   in the bath.

Reading

Ask students to listen with their books closed as you read the selection aloud. Go through it a second time with books open and the students following along. A third time select students at random to take turns reading aloud, one sentence per student.

In line 7, point out the expression *to stay home.* The preposition *at* is not necessary.

Extract 1 *(Dos Santos 1983:73)*

Extract 2 (*Stannard Allen, El-Anani, and Sabah 1973:7*)

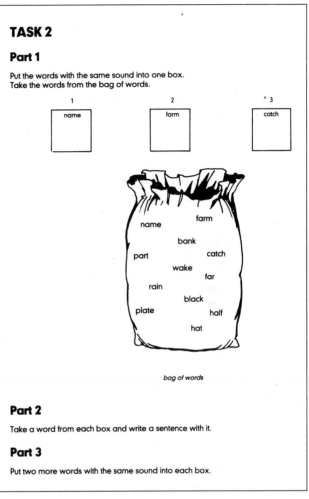

Extract 3 (*Molteno Project 1987:2*)

In Extract 2 the learner is faced with sets of words which are built up from letters already presented. It is implied that a skill such as word recognition develops sequentially with the learner progressing through a series of stages as letters, followed by those same letters in various combinations, are presented to them. Moreover, the letters and words presented for sight recognition do not seem to relate to those selected for the accompanying writing practice. Extract 1, in recommending that students read aloud different sentences of a short reading passage already read to them by the teacher, highlights the skill of reading aloud with, presumably, an acceptable pronunciation rather than assessing the learner's ability to process continuous unfamiliar text. The task in Extract 3 asks the learner to discriminate and group words which rhyme with each other.

While these activities are product oriented in that they focus on the achievement of a specified task, they do not necessarily preclude a process approach in the classroom. This might be exemplified, for instance, if when using the task in Extract 3, the teacher showed an interest in the children's criteria for classifying the words and discussed these with them in the course of completing the task, rather than being concerned merely to note 'correct' answers.

A rather different case could be made for the task in Extract 2. Arguably, it is helpful to build up a basic sight vocabulary of decontextualized but phonetically regular words, especially when, as is the case for these Arab learners of English, they are being introduced to a new writing system. Skills teaching of this kind offers one way of grading the language input.

However there may be problems with a focus on the teaching of specific skills. First, as noted in **6.2**, research has failed to establish any hierarchy of skills through which one progresses to become an increasingly effective reader. Also, in the case of early reading in particular, the skills taught may relate only marginally, if at all, to the activity of reading. For instance, the sight recognition of words such as 'fob' or 'fin' does not necessarily promote the ability to make sense of a written text where such words are likely to make only a very rare appearance and to take on variable meanings in context. Equally, the ability to decode written language phonetically may not facilitate the reading of continuous or contextualized text in English. One reason, as explained in **2.1**, is that English is only partially phonetically based. This means that, even if children have learned to match up phonemes and graphemes, this knowledge will only help them some of the time. Good young learners (for example those already reading with some fluency by the age of five) will rarely be observed to use phonic decoding. It is likely that they have come to realize that there are other more effective ways of processing print. As noted in Wallace (1988), phonics is very much a hit and miss affair, in particular for early learners, as they are not in a position to know with which new words a phonic decoding approach will pay off.

Moreover, an emphasis on phonics is, in many ways, even less appropriate for second language than for first language learners. First, if they can already read in their first language, they will have mastered the principles by which spoken language relates to written. What may help the second language learner, especially if his or her first language is more phonetically regular than English, is an understanding of ways in which regularities in the English writing system are more systematically represented by visual features alone than any connection between sound and visual symbol, as discussed in **2.1**. These features of written English can be pointed out and discussed in the course of reading (for example in one-to-one reading with a teacher) rather than being specifically taught.

In the more unusual case of second language learners who are illiterate in their first language, there are several reasons against a heavy emphasis on phonics. First, their spoken English is likely to have sets of homophones which are different from those of Standard English. If, for instance, in their own spoken English they do not discriminate between 'pin' and 'pen' they may not hear the difference when these and other pairs are presented in 'drilling' activities. However this difficulty in sound discrimination will not necessarily affect their reading for sense any more than in the case of learners who speak a non-standard variety of English and who also have sets of homophones which are different from those of Standard English. Secondly, in emphasizing the graphophonic level of language to the exclusion of the semantic and syntactic levels, we may fail to encourage students to use the whole range of their linguistic and schematic resources to predict meaning when faced with continuous written text.

7.4 Reading strategies

What are the alternatives to skills approaches? It might be preferable to talk not of teaching specific *skills* but of developing reading *strategies*. A strategy-based approach assumes, as argued in **6**, that reading is a unitary process which cannot be subdivided into constituent skills. Strategies involve ways of processing text which will vary with the nature of the text, the reader's purpose, and the context of situation.

Early learners can be encouraged to explore features of written English through experience with the language itself rather than being taught 'about the language'. One approach which allows learners to try out their strategies for making sense of written English is that offered by the *Breakthrough to Literacy* material. Learners are given sets of words and blank cards on which to add new words of their own. They then create their own sentences on a 'sentence builder'. This sentence-making activity draws learners' attention to key features of English syntax such as word order: it also offers opportunities for word building through the provision of cards featuring morphemes such as 's' and the '-ed' inflectional ending. In the *Breakthrough* approach, rather than being explicitly taught, the learner is allowed to experiment with sentence building and the teacher is at hand to guide and adjust this exploration. A resource like the sentence builder allows the teacher to establish and build on the second language learner's existing knowledge of English lexis and syntax.

Another feature of classrooms centred more on facilitating learning processes than on teaching specific skills is the use made of environmental print. This includes letters, forms, and a range of signs, notices, and labels of the kind found in out-of-school contexts such as the street or local supermarket. Moreover, if we accept that the classroom is a community in its own right (see **3.3**), then exposure to a wide range of written English genres can be offered even in classrooms in non-English-speaking countries. Included in the material may be books, not only books written by educators to teach the language or teach reading, but those written by authors to inform, instruct, and entertain.

Once reading of continuous text begins, the strategy-oriented teacher will be as concerned to observe readers in the course of reading as to assess outcomes in the form of answers to the comprehension questions which generally follow a reading task. He or she is likely to be interested not merely in the surface fluency with which a text is rendered aloud, but also in the nature of miscues, or, with silent reading, the reader's own perception of problems during the reading process (see the discussion in 6). In this sense a strategic approach to the teaching of reading demonstrates interest in processes as much as products, that is what goes on during reading itself as well as the nature of goals and outcomes.

One starting point for the development of strategy-based approaches is to consider what good readers do—whether experienced or in the early stages of learning—in the course of reading, particularly when confronted with textual difficulties such as unknown words. We looked very generally at the strategies of experienced first language readers in Section One. The strategies of early second language readers have been considered in more detail in a series of studies by Hosenfeld (for example 1977 and 1984) who worked on the principle that, by looking at what good learners do, less successful learners might be helped. High and low scorers on a reading proficiency test were asked to report on their own strategies as they read aloud foreign language texts. The successful readers tended to select from a range of strategies. For example, they skipped inessential words, guessed from context, read in broad phrases, and continued reading the text where they were unsuccessful in decoding a word or phrase. Similar strategies can also be observed to characterize the reading of good young first language readers (Wallace 1988).

▶ TASK 33

Below are transcripts of four young learner readers reading aloud a simple text. The first two are very young first language readers, both aged five. The second two are second language readers who are both aged eleven and have been in Britain for about five years. Which strategies, used by them in dealing with unknown words, do you think are the most effective?

Kate: The golden sapiel wagged his tail—spaniel wagged his tail

Claire: Grandma took baby—I'll start again—Grandma took baby through the crowd

Kuldip: He sailed on T–I double L—tall one day he came to the island of Emeralds

Maqsood: Linda is sixteen and works in a toy shop. Kids—kinds st . . . kinds staffs thinks Harry [the text reads 'kids stuff', thinks Harry].

Kate and Claire display several of the positive reading strategies described by Hosenfeld, respectively going ahead in the text to gain more context, filling in with a nonsense word in the meantime, or, in Claire's case, backtracking in order to read the text as a larger chunk. Kuldip and Maqsood are reading more slowly and with greater hesitation (though this cannot be captured in the transcript) and attend to more local features of the text, attempting to name the letters or sound out unfamiliar words, possibly drawing on their experience of skills oriented reading instruction of the kind described in 7.3. There is also some evidence from empirical studies (see Wallace 1988) that young second language readers focus more than do first language learners on graphophonic features in the text. This lends weight to the case for the teacher to help extend the range of such learners' strategies.

Good learners, in short, tend to use the same strategies as good experienced readers, drawing on as much of the surrounding text as possible, being prepared to tolerate uncertainty, using a wide range of textual cues in predicting what comes next, and generally being flexible in their response to texts (see 6.2). The teacher, by watching the various ways in which his or her learners process texts, can encourage the use of those strategies which are observed to be most effective.

One role of the teacher is to judge how and when his or her own interventions might support an early reader when reading aloud. Thus, rather than simply 'hearing learners read' and focusing on how they pronounce the words, teacher and learners might profit from sharing their knowledge of particular topics and discussing the salient features of particular genres in the actual course of reading.

▶ TASK 34

Consider these two interactions between teacher and learner, where the learner is reading aloud to the teacher. What differences can you observe in the nature of the interactions?

1 Vijay, aged six, is reading a story called 'Karen at the Zoo':

Vijay	*teacher*
She went to the cocolile	You know that word don't you
and the big fish	What do you think the keeper was going to do with the fish?
eat it	He was going to eat it? It was the crocodile that was going to eat it

2 Manjula, an eight-year-old, is reading this text aloud to her teacher:

Manjula	*teacher*
One day Ugly Boy came running	
into the house. He said	
Grandmother, I am hungry,	
I am going out to pick some	
nuts. I am not afraid of the old bear	'the old bear'
	Can you say that?
the old bear	

Vijay's teacher encourages him to interpret the picture as related to the text and is keen to engage in an interaction around the text. As Manjula had made no error in her reading, her teacher would appear to be intervening merely to correct her pronunciation, in this way encouraging a clearly articulated 'reading aloud' style.

One opportunity offered by the shared reading situation, where there is active discussion about both the content and the language of the text, is that learners are encouraged to develop a *metalanguage*, a way of talking about features of written texts which can help to heighten awareness of what is involved in the processing of written language. Thus there may be discussion of form, for example the systematic incidence of the '-ed' morpheme in regular past tense verbs, but in the context of the processing of continuous text rather than during a grammar lesson.

Moreover, shared reading situations, where teacher and learner or pairs and groups of learners discuss texts and their own reading styles, also offer the opportunity for the development of what are known as *metacognitive strategies*, by which the learner displays awareness of his or her own reading strategies and learning processes more generally. Questions which can promote the development of this kind of awareness are those which directly ask learners what they typically do when confronted with textual difficulty. In short, both metalinguistic and metacognitive abilities can be developed in the process of shared reading.

7.5 What do skills and strategies approaches look like?

It may be easier to understand skills and strategies approaches to early reading if we look at some teacher–learner situations and examine more closely what teachers actually do in the classroom rather than what educators and researchers say about the teaching of reading.

▶ TASK 35

The examples here are taken from classrooms in three different English-speaking countries where the teacher is teaching young children. Consider how far the three reading events seem to embody either a skills or a strategies approach.

1 Mrs Graham is teaching a large class of small children using a 'big book', that is a large-format book with print big enough to share with the whole class. Mrs Graham invites the children's participation in a number of ways; she asks them to comment on the title and author for instance, and to predict the events of the story from the picture. As they progress through the text she asks for further predictions as to what is most likely to happen next.

2 Mrs Charles is teaching initial reading in an ESL class. She is practising the short vowels. The children play a game which involves each of two teams guessing which is the short vowel in a series of simple monosyllabic words such as 'ship', 'sheep' and 'cut', 'cute'.

3 In Miss Smith's class there are a number of pairs of children around the room. Her own group of twelve-year-olds are reading to five-year-olds who have been brought from the kindergarten class for this purpose.

Each of these situations reveals a different view of the reading process on the teacher's part. Mrs Charles takes a view of learning to read as a set of skills—being able to pronounce and to discriminate between particular sounds is considered to be a prerequisite of reading. Mrs Graham takes a more context based approach, using a full text, albeit one designed with a didactic purpose, and involving the children in considering factors about whole books such as author and title. She sees a strong story-line which encourages prediction as a route to reading rather than any specific practice with individual items of language. Mrs Graham opts not to break down texts into smaller chunks, nor to ask the children to work on specific skills. Her encouragement of prediction involves the children using all the cueing systems available to them, most importantly the more global ones to do with predicting outcomes in the story, by drawing on their schemas for the story genre of the kind discussed in 5.

Miss Smith attends to the whole situation in which reading and learning to read takes place. In other words, she has seen the importance not just of offering children access to the broad *textual* context but of the context of *situation* in early reading, that is, who is reading to whom in what particular setting, as discussed in 3.

Approaches which promote the use of whole texts and an awareness of whole situational contexts as supports for early literacy have come to be known, in the United States, as 'whole language' views of language and literacy learning (see, for example, Goodman, Bridges Bird, and Goodman: *The Whole Language Catalog* 1991). In Britain these approaches draw on a tradition in primary school education of child-centred and integrated views of learning. The implications of such approaches are, first, that one begins with the child's existing knowledge and learning experiences and, second, that one acknowledges that there may be diverse but equally legitimate out-of-school literacy experiences which children bring with them to school, as noted in **3**.

It also means that reading will be seen not as an isolated activity but a mode that is inevitably integrated with speaking, writing, and listening. Thus listening to stories is a very good way of acquiring an understanding of their typical structure and content. Talking about them will clarify their meanings, and writing your own will help to reinforce a sense of how stories take shape and offer insight into the roles of writers and readers.

7.6 Links with later reading strategies

A strategy based approach implies a continuity between early and more advanced reading. A key principle for both is that, as argued in **6**, we read selectively and flexibly: in other words, we read different texts in different ways which are related to the function of the text and our own purpose in reading it in a particular context. Effective readers of all levels of ability will scan for specific information, skim to get an initial overview of a text, and be prepared to read and re-read with greater attention those parts of the text which are of particular relevance to their purpose. At the same time, they will see reading as a process by which meanings are not simply extracted from the text, but mediated by the linguistic and schematic knowledge which they bring to it.

In the classroom a reading lesson might try to reflect this process in the following way: prior to reading the text there might be various kinds of pre-reading activities, or discussion of shared expectations about the topic or genre of a text to be read, perhaps drawn from the title, or pictures related to it. During the process of reading, prompts may be offered to encourage learners to articulate the kind of information which can be drawn from the text, and from their own current knowledge of the world. With early learners these may be part of a dialogue between teacher and learners about 'what may happen next'. In the case of inter-mediate and advanced readers, whether reading in a first or second language, there are also pre-reading and while-reading procedures which can encourage the activation of linguistic and schematic knowledge. These are discussed in **10** and **11**.

Ultimately however, the success of classroom reading activities will also depend on a number of other factors. This is because classroom learning processes are social as much as individual, involving complex interactions between learners and between learners and teachers. They are also affected by the wider circumstances in which learning takes place. In **8** we will take a more detailed look at the range of learning contexts, roles, and purposes of second language learner readers.

8 The learning context: roles and purposes of second language learners

At this point we will consider in more detail who the learner is, what kind of educational and language background he or she has, and, in particular, what purpose he or she has in learning to read in English.

The contexts of learning and the roles and purposes of learners within these will clearly vary considerably. For instance, some second language learners will be integrated with groups of first language learners, especially young learners acquiring literacy through the medium of English as their second language. This was the case with Vijay and Manjula in Task 34. Others will have very specific reading needs in the second language and may be learning the language in near isolation from native speakers.

8.1 The social roles and context of learning of the second language learner

The social roles of the second language learner will relate to the social context of learning which can be characterized in terms of the three levels of context which we discussed in 4. First, what is the immediate context of learning? Is it a formal or an informal classroom setting? Is it an English speaking environment or not? Then we might consider the institutional context related, for instance, to typical educational practices adopted in the teaching of subjects across the curriculum. One question to consider here may be the most favoured approach to first language reading instruction. What view of reading is suggested by the materials available in the classroom, and the prevailing methodology? Is the emphasis on the teaching of specific skills or the development and extension of existing learning strategies? Prevailing views on first language reading education will in turn affect the way in which the learners perceive the function of second language literacy.

Educational practices in schools will reflect social structures in the wider society. If, for instance, social roles are clearly defined and stratified, this may mean that it would be seen to be inappropriate for students to challenge authority. This would include challenging the perceived authority of texts, and maybe teachers' judgements and interpretations, in the ways discussed in Section One of this book. In short, it is helpful, when proposing new teaching approaches, to take account of the diverse learning contexts of second language learners, in particular their educational and language background, as well as their accustomed roles as learners and their learning purposes.

► TASK 36

Note some of the factors which might affect the development of English language literacy for these four learners, all in English language classes.

1 Giovanni is aged twelve and beginning to study English at Scuola Media in Italy; he has had little contact with English other than in pop songs. He reads well in Italian.

2 Wang is aged eight, in an ESL class in Britain. He can read a little in Chinese. He came to England from Hong Kong a year ago.

3 Rainer is a German engineer, aged twenty-eight, studying English in Germany. He is highly educated but speaks no English at all.

4 Amna is Pakistani, aged nineteen; she is fairly fluent in English but had no schooling in Pakistan and does not read in her mother-tongue which is Urdu. She cannot read in English either.

Let us first take the case of Wang. How far will he be able to draw on his first language literacy in learning to read in English? Much depends again on our view of the learning to read process. If we see it as the learning of skills, then it might be argued that Wang needs specific instruction in the principles behind the English writing system, which are clearly different from the Chinese; if we see it as a unitary process involving strategies which are generalizable across languages, then Wang already knows what reading is.

Amna is illiterate and therefore a crucial issue arises. Should she be encouraged to acquire literacy in her mother-tongue first? In most cases this allows learners to begin to learn to read in naturalistic contexts, for example they need to make sense of environmental print, including print in the home and family setting. Moreover Cummins (1979) argues that a firm foundation of first language competence accompanied by first language literacy is the best route into second language acquisition of oral and written language modes. However, there are conflicting factors here, among which are access to print in the first language, and attitudinal and motivational factors. Most of the print in Amna's new environment is in English. This means that if English-medium literacy is used, there is support from naturally occurring print outside the classroom. In addition, Amna perceives English as the high status language, access to which will give her a job and a chance of further education. Certainly first language literacy will have very important symbolic functions and there will be strong motivation to acquire this (see Wallace and Goodman 1989). However, in many cases second language learners, both children such as

Vijay and Manjula, and young adults in circumstances such as Amna's, acquire initial literacy through English. They then frequently move on to develop literacy in their mother-tongue, a process which will be supported by their second language literacy.

Giovanni and Rainer are learning English outside an English speaking environment. Most of their contact with English in its spoken form is in the classroom. However, while naturally occurring speech events may be hard to come upon, both will have ready access to written English language material outside the classroom in the form of, for example, English language newspapers and novels. In other words, they can have extensive contact with print outside the context of classroom learning.

Giovanni and Rainer have another advantage. They can already read. Most researchers have conceded that second language learners who are highly literate, especially in related languages, are enormously advantaged. Indeed learning the language can often take place primarily through the medium of print, though the level of general second language proficiency which needs to be reached before reading strategies can be successfully transferred to the second language is a subject of continuing debate and research (as discussed, for example, in Alderson and Urquhart 1984 and Carrell 1991).

Rainer, unlike Giovanni, has a very specific purpose in learning to read in English. He needs to deal with specialist texts as English is the language most commonly used in international dealings in the multinational firm he works for. Much of his reading will be in the area of what is known as ESP, English for Specific Purposes, which we turn to next.

8.2 Reading for specific purposes

Many students learn English for a very particular purpose and terms such as ESP and EAP (English for Academic Purposes) have become common. ESP learning is usually related to particular content areas such as engineering or medicine. And for such students it is often reading knowledge of the specialist area rather than proficiency in any of the other modes which is perceived as important.

In the early days of ESP, applied linguists took the view that there were important differences between, say, the English of commerce and that of physics. On this basis it was reasonable to argue that texts should be selected from the learners' specialist area. Learners, would then, it was claimed, see the content of the text as relevant in the way that general texts were not, and would therefore be more motivated to read them.

One difficulty with the attempt to tailor text choice very closely to learner need is in defining the exact features which characterize subject-specific texts. The view that there are specific 'engineering' texts, as opposed to 'medical' ones for instance, has long been challenged. As Hutchinson and Waters (1985) observe, analyses of texts ultimately failed to show convincingly that there was a distinctive syntax, lexis, or organizational pattern in texts in specific subject areas. Attention therefore shifted to the conceptual and communicative features of specialist texts which, it was argued, cut across the traditional subject boundaries. That is, interest centred on the way key ideas in texts were communicated across a range of topics.

For instance, Johns and Davies (1983) identified a 'physical structure' type of text which may be about such unrelated topics as a flowering plant, a skeleton, or a suspension bridge. In each case, claim Johns and Davies, this type of text consistently provides information which falls into the following categories:

1 the parts of the structure
2 the properties or attributes of the parts
3 the location of the parts
4 the function of the parts

The authors of one well-known reading series, *Reading and Thinking in English*, are interested both in the propositional relations within texts and also in the communicative functions which characterize academic discourse. As Henry Widdowson puts it in his preface to one of the books, *Discovering Discourse*, the topics are selected 'to demonstrate the communicative functions of English which are common in a whole range of academic writing'. The kind of functions included are: 'to give instructions', 'to describe', 'to report events', and 'to generalize'.

► TASK 37

What function is exemplified by these two texts?

The camera and the eye are similar in many respects. They both need light rays in order to function. Both have a sensitive surface on which the image is formed. In the eye the image is formed on the retina. In the camera the image is formed on the film. As in a camera, the image on the retina is inverted.

Both the eye and the camera have a lens. The lens focuses the image on the sensitive surface. In the camera, the lens moves backwards and forwards. In the eye the curvature of the lens is changed. In this respect the eye differs from the camera.

Both the camera and the eye have a device to regulate the amount of light that passes through the lens. In the camera there is a shutter of variable speed and a diaphragm of variable aperture. In the eye the iris automatically adjusts the size of the pupil according to the intensity of light.

Both the eye and the camera are sensitive to light, shade and colour. The film records light, shade and colour. The eye perceives them but does not record them. The two eyes together produce a three-dimensional image. The camera lens produces a two-dimensional image.

The eye is more flexible than the camera. It can adapt more quickly to a wider range of light conditions. Both the camera and the eye can register small objects and distant objects. The camera performs these functions better than the eye.

Text 1 (*Reading and Thinking in English* 1979:90–1)

Social insects live in integrated communities which in some ways are similar to human communities. In both types of community there is division of labour. In insect societies certain insects are responsible for reproduction; the workers collect food while the soldiers defend the colony. In the same way human groups such as farmers and shopkeepers have specialized functions in producing goods and providing services to the community.

Insect and human societies are also alike in that individual members of the community work together. Termite workers co-ordinate their efforts to build nests. Similarly, in human societies engineers, architects, town planners and construction workers unite to build cities.

The nests of social insects are as complex as a man-made city. In some insect nests special accommodation is provided for the young and for food storage. Many nests also have devices for regulating the temperature. So insect nests are as functional as human houses.

It is not surprising, therefore, that many analogies have been made between social insects and human societies. It must not be forgotten, however, that insect social behaviour is determined by innate instinctive mechanisms. Insects show no capacity for learning or for developing a social tradition based on learning.

Text 2 (*Reading and Thinking in English 1979:94*)

It is fairly clear that, although the topics are very different, both texts share the function of making comparisons. Functions are here defined less in terms of the communicative intent of a whole text within a social context than in terms of the way language is used to express a particular concept at one point within a larger text. Recent work on genre, notably by Swales (1990), aims to bring in a stronger sociocultural perspective by looking at some of the culture-specific factors which make a text recognizable as serving a particular function. He thus extends the scope of communicative function to include some of the features discussed in Section One of this book. He notes how a genre can change over time, drawing on different kinds of conventions of use. One example he gives is the way in which articles in journals now, as compared with twenty years ago, seem to require a much greater number of references, tend to be organized differently, for instance with subheadings, and are more likely to be co-authored.

What all the more recent trends in ESP seem to share is the assumption that reader strategies can be generalized across subject boundaries. Attention has shifted from a narrow focus on specific purpose texts to a broader consideration of the features typical of all texts written for formal, academic purposes. Johns and Davies (1983) point out that the student who is to become a teacher of English, or is already a teacher of English attending a Master's or Diploma level course, has as much of a specific purpose in learning English as have doctors or engineers. What all are likely to share is difficulty in reading formal prose, a difficulty, what is more, which they may also have in reading similar texts in their first language. This would be consistent with the view of reading which sees it as involving generalizable strategies across languages and situations rather than specific skills.

A further point related to academic writing, a high prestige variety, is that students may need to be helped to resist deference to the text (see our discussion in 6). Some writing is not easily comprehensible, including that of established writers, and many of the difficulties which foreign learners have with academic texts are shared by native speaker readers. It is important to note that these difficulties may not be the readers' fault. Indeed one is bound to wonder, at times, whether some texts are designed to be difficult to understand. Andersen (1988) quotes one piece of research which suggested that the more prestigious the journal the more difficult it was to read. That this was not because of the inherent complexity of the ideas expressed was at least partly tested by producing a simpler version of the original texts. The style was made easier by cutting out unnecessary words, substituting easy for difficult words, and breaking up long sentences. The academics who were asked to judge the simpler versions in all cases rated the simpler rewrites less highly than the syntactically more complex ones.

8.3 Reading for general purposes

Even in the case of a very clearly defined specific need, students of English will still need and want to be general readers. The importance of a broad diet of texts cannot be overstated. Dubin (1989) noted how as soon as her ESP students, primarily social science majors in the United States, put aside their social psychology textbook to do some related general interest reading, they encountered difficulties which were largely connected with the demands made on the reader's background knowledge. It is exactly this background knowledge which can be developed concurrently with more specialist knowledge if a wide range of genres and topics is included from the early stages of an ESP reading course.

Finally, while second language learners will have varying roles and purposes in reading, they will also have much in common with each other and with first language learners. One shared goal will be the wish to read for pleasure in the second language. This was mentioned in 1 as a key factor in allowing people to develop fluency as readers and has been a major guiding principle of the strategy-based approaches described in 7. One of the aims of these approaches is to provide opportunities, even for beginner readers, to read a wide range of interesting material.

8.4 Reading for pleasure in the second language

Students asked to mention their reading preferences in English can give some surprising answers. Tsai, a Chinese student, reads Geoffrey Archer, a popular writer of fiction which often features political intrigue. Nuntaga, from Thailand, favours the *Readers Digest* (a popular choice) and fairy tales. Ketut, from Indonesia, even though he is following quite an advanced teacher education course, goes for simplified versions of the classics. Others in Ketut's group mentioned Barbara Cartland, a writer of romantic fiction. Most active readers, in any language, include thrillers, romantic fiction, or comics in their diet of reading. Second language learners can be encouraged to read for entertainment in this way, that is to read material other than what is usually considered 'quality' literature. A random and catholic exposure to written texts offers a linguistic and schematic base for more demanding reading of good contemporary fiction, the classics, and academic and specialist texts. Students can be encouraged to take account of their existing preferences. If they enjoy science fiction in their first language then they are likely to enjoy similar material in the second language. They will, of course, also have experience with the genre which will help them to predict many features of the second language text. At the same time, cross-cultural genres contain culture-specific discourses, and these can be explored and discussed.

Moreover, if we take an interactive view of reading as described in 6, readers can invest even very simple texts with complexity. Literature in particular offers this potential. Material which is linguistically simple may invite complex interpretations, that is, the demands made on the reader may be aesthetic and intellectual rather than linguistic. This applies particularly to poetry. Some of the finest poems in English are linguistically accessible. Their depth and complexity often lie in ambiguities which second language as well as first language learners can explore and enjoy. This explains the continuing popularity of such poems as Robert Frost's 'Stopping by Woods on a Snowy Evening' (see Widdowson 1975 for an analysis of this poem). This kind of text invites a wide range of interpretations and is likely to relate to universal aspects of the human condition, such as love and death, rather than culture-specific topics.

However some literary texts do reflect contemporary values in the writer's culture and make quite specific and topical references. They can for this reason offer succinct and pithy insights into features of the target culture's value-systems and life-style.

▶ TASK 38

The writer of the poems on page 70 is a contemporary British black poet. She describes what it is like to be black, female, and fat in a white, male—and thin—world. Could this or similar literary material be used in your teaching context?

The Fat Black Woman Composes a Black Poem . . .

Black as the intrusion
of a rude wet tongue

Black as the boldness
of a quick home run

Black as the blackness
of a rolling ship

Black as the sweetness
of black orchid milk

Black as the token
of my ancestors bread

Black as the beauty
of the nappy head

Black as the blueness
of a swift backlash

Black as the spraying
of a reggae sunsplash

. . . And a Fat Poem

Fat is
as fat is
as fat is

Fat does
as fat thinks

Fat feels
as fat please

Fat believes

     Fat is to butter
     as milk is to cream
     fat is to sugar
     as pud is to steam

Fat is a dream
in times of lean

     fat is a darling
     a dumpling
     a squeeze
     fat is cuddles
     up a baby's sleeve

     and fat speaks for itself

(*Nichols 1984:16–17*)

9 The role of the text in the second language classroom

One advantage of texts such as the poems introduced in 8 is that they are short and can therefore be memorized and continually reused by being written up on a blackboard. This is an important factor where access to second language reading material is restricted. Some teachers and learners will be in environments where a wide variety of English language material is readily available in the form of newspapers, magazines, and books. Others will need to be more resourceful in acquiring a supply of reading matter for both their own use and as class material for their learners.

9.1 Criteria for selecting material

Assuming that there is a reasonably wide range of potential material available, what factors are in play when we consider criteria for selecting texts for our students?

► TASK 39

1 Which of the following criteria do you think are most important in choosing texts in the foreign or second language classroom?
2 In what ways are these criteria affected by the learners' language level?

The text:
- should be a vehicle for teaching specific language structure and vocabulary.
- should offer the opportunity to promote key reading strategies.
- should present content which is familiar and of interest to the learners.
- should be at the appropriate language level.
- should be authentic, that is a naturally occurring text, not specially written for pedagogic purposes.
- should be exploitable in the classroom, that is, lead to a range of classroom activities.

Clearly these criteria are not necessarily mutually exclusive. We are likely to be guided by more than one of them when we select texts. To start with

I shall consider some of the issues raised by the first three criteria, that is the extent to which we focus on, respectively, the structures within the text, ways of reading the text, and the topic or subject matter of the text. I shall then move on to consider how we can reconcile the need for linguistic simplicity with authenticity. Ways of exploiting texts in the classroom will be discussed in 10 and 11.

The text as a vehicle for teaching language structure and vocabulary
First there are what we might call 'language focused' texts. These are sometimes justified for classroom use on the grounds that they are not primarily for reading at all but are exponents of the structure of the language—what Widdowson (1978) has called 'usage' rather than 'use'. The majority of these texts are written specifically to 'teach the language' in that they make certain key features of the language system visible through the repetition of particular structures or lexis.

▶ TASK 40

This is a text taken from a beginners' coursebook. Typically it is accompanied by, and relates to, a picture.

What do you think is the role of this kind of text in the language classroom?

Figure 2   Typical structuralist/behaviourist material

25 At the cinema

Peter's standing outside the cinema. He's waiting for Lulu, his girlfriend, and he's looking at his watch because she's late. An old man's coming out of the cinema. A young man's going into the cinema. A boy's running up the steps. A woman's buying a ticket from the cashier. Some people are queueing outside the cinema.

Questions

Where's Peter standing?
Who's he waiting for?
What's he looking at?
Why is he looking at his watch?
Who's coming out of the cinema?
Who's going into the cinema?
Who's buying a ticket?
Where are the people queueing?

(*Hartley and Viney 1978,* quoted by *Williams 1984:14*)

Though they are often introduced as 'reading' texts, texts of this kind are not typical of the kind of language we normally read. They do not conform to the basic conventions of written language either formally or functionally: it is difficult, for instance, to allocate a communicative function to such texts. The aim of the written text is in fact not so much to teach sentence patterns as to reinforce sentence patterns already intensively practised in their spoken form. As Williams (1984:15) notes: 'it is difficult to imagine anyone reading this text for either information or interest—the real reason for reading is to learn language.'

A slightly different approach is to focus not on the sentence patterns within texts but the kinds of cohesive features, introduced in **2.1**, which allow us to recognize stretches of written language as texts. One can use any text to highlight ways in which written texts are cohesive by focusing on features of structure within or beyond sentences such as pronoun reference or logical connectors. There is no need to specially write a text as cohesion is a necessary feature of all texts. However we may wish, for pedagogic purposes, to adapt a text so as to present learners with a higher frequency of these features.

► **TASK 41**

In the extract below, questions are put in the margin alongside the text. How useful is this as a way of drawing learners' attention to features of reference in texts?

Complete the following

one refers to _____?

there refers to _____?

which refers to _____?

It is AD 79. People live on the green hills surrounding Mount Vesuvius. Vesuvius is a volcano★, but *one* which has been sleeping for hundreds of years. The people who live *there* remember a terrible earthquake★ *which* happened seventeen years before. But in the rich trading town of Pompeii and among the vineyards, it is easy to forget. On 24 August the mountain explodes. The vineyards are covered with lava. The cities of Pompeii and Stabiae are buried in ashes. Mud destroys the city of Herculaneum. It is the

it refers to _____?

end of a civilisation★, and no one expected *it* to happen.

In August AD 79 Mount _____ and ended _____.

No one _____.

(*Ellis and Ellis 1983:21*)

Early learners of English, especially if they are not literate in their first language, may need some help with the way reference is used in written texts (see the discussion in **2.1** relating to pronoun reference). For more advanced learners, literate in their first and possibly other languages as well, reference features might be focused on more selectively to draw attention to differences between their first language and English, for example the ways in which reference to new and given information is signalled. Moreover, different genres exhibit different kinds of reference as we noted in Task 19; one kind of text-focused activity is to ask learners to consider the role which reference and other cohesive devices play in the construction of different genres.

In general, there is a case for text focused activities of the kind in Task 41. As suggested in **2.1** and **7**, novice readers need to acquire some understanding of the formal elements which relate to the structure of words, clauses, and whole texts; they need, in particular, to be helped to make the key connections between spoken and written English.

Texts which teach language through reading

Another possibility, expressed by the second criterion in Task 39, is that we select texts, not for any distinctive linguistic features, but because they promote reading. This is in line with the principle that language is developed in the course of reading itself. Elley (1984) on finding that a number of studies of Fijian second language learners indicated very poor competence in reading, suggested two likely causes: first, there was a general lack of availability of childrens' books in any language, due partly to the fact that Fijian teachers did not see reading as a way of learning language; second, and related to the first point, the English language instructional programme used in the elementary schools in Fiji was based on a highly structured audiolingual approach which played down reading as a source of language learning. Elley concluded that the delay in introducing written language denied the learners crucial exposure to English and that language is learned largely through reading. He was describing a situation where English is the medium of instruction; a study in progress (Brusch 1991), modelled on Elley's is looking at how the English language proficiency of German secondary school students will be influenced by an extensive reading programme which is based on the simple principle of making available to the students large numbers of books written both for first and foreign language learners of English.

If it is indeed the case that we learn the language through reading, we can select texts not for their potential as vehicles of structures or lexis, but for their potential in developing reading strategies. Certain kinds of texts, for instance, may lend themselves to scanning, and others to skimming, as we discuss more fully in **10**.

The more fluently and widely the second language reader reads, the more exposure to the key structures and vocabulary of the second language he or she gains. Elley (1984) found that Fijian and Indian children were able to determine the meanings of large numbers of unfamiliar English structures when presented in the context of meaningful written sentences. This indicates that structures do not have to be in the active repertoire of learners to be understood in reading. My work with adult learners becoming literate through English as their second language (Wallace 1988) confirms Elley's findings. It follows that wide access to meaningful written language may be an effective way of learning new structures and not just of reinforcing or practising known ones, even for early second or foreign language readers. Written language is generally more fully structured and more consistent, as well as being more permanent, than speech. This means that key features of the language are visible and open to review in a way that they are not in spoken language. It also means that if we want to motivate learners to read widely in the second language, the overall content of the texts we select will be more important than specific linguistic features.

Texts which offer high-interest content
This brings us to the third broad criterion in selecting texts introduced in Task 39, that of the text's content. Put simply, the text must be interesting enough for the learner to want to read it. This issue of interest is a difficult one. Clearly there will be considerable individual differences as well as preferences shared by groups of learners. Nonetheless it may be possible to identify texts which are inherently motivating.

▶ **TASK 42**

Consider the opening lines of the texts below, all from English language teaching materials. Is it possible to predict which might be of the greatest general interest to your learners?

1 First let me tell you something about the way we work and what we are paid. There are two kinds of work—regular, that is salary work, and piecework. The regular work pays about $6 a week and the girls have to be at their machines at 7 o'clock in the morning and they stay at them until 8 o'clock at night, with just one-half hour for lunch in that time.
(quoted in *Auerbach and Wallerstein 1987:71*)

2 Joanne works for the Lincoln Company. There are two shifts in the Lincoln Company, a day shift and a night shift. Joanne works the day shift. Her schedule is Tuesday through Saturday from 8 o'clock to 5 pm. Her lunch time is 12.00 noon to 1.00 pm.
(*Savage, How, and Yeung 1982:164*)

3 Many, many years ago there was a very rich landlord who owned a lot of land and houses.
(*Stannard Allen, El-Anani, and Salah 1972:59*)

These are all extremely simple texts linguistically. However, we might agree that something about their content makes us more interested in reading on in Texts 1 and 3 than in Text 2. For a start, Text 3 signals the beginning of a recognizable kind of narrative, thus allowing us to engage with the text by activating a relevant schema. Even between Texts 1 and 2, where the content is similar, Text 1 is likely to hold more interest for more people. Firstly, the genre is more readily identifiable as that of 'true-life story' (of the working conditions of women factory workers at the start of the century). This is indicated by the direct address of the reader by the writer. In Text 2, although the textbook from which it comes instructs the reader to 'read the story' the text is not, in fact, what we usually understand as a 'story'. We expect stories to narrate events which are newsworthy and to have recognizable beginnings such as in Text 3. Moreover, in Text 2, unlike in Text 1, the events are, for most readers, unexceptional. It is not unusual for example, for people to have a lunch time from noon to 1.00 pm whereas it is, in most countries, now unusual for people to work a twelve-and-a-half hour day.

9.2 Simple versus authentic texts

It is often assumed that authentic texts are generally more interesting than those written for a pedagogic purpose. If we accept for the moment that this is the case, how can we reconcile the requirements of authenticity and high-interest content with those of linguistic accessibility, especially when selecting texts for early and intermediate readers?

Let us take the issues of simplicity and authenticity in turn.

9.3 Assessing text difficulty

For many learners fully authentic texts may be linguistically too complex, and it is therefore worth considering the role of simplified material in the foreign language classroom, whether this is specially prepared by the teacher or takes the form of published material. First we will look at the work which has been done under the broad heading of 'readability studies', in other words, what factors make a text difficult in particular for a foreign learner, and when is it therefore appropriate to consider some kind of simplification?

What makes a text difficult?
A view inherent in much material for both early native speaker and foreign language learner readers is that written texts are difficult if they contain a certain number of unknown words.

There are several problems with this approach to text difficulty. One relates to what we understand by a 'new' or 'unknown' word. On my computer screen as I write there is the familiar word 'menu'. However, this word will be 'new' in its specific computer sense to someone who is not computer literate. Moreover, even in the rare event where a particular word is very powerfully associated with one meaning, words are not learned once and for all; meaning its built up around a word with each successive encounter with that word in context.

This leads on to another factor, namely that words are learned in context, written contexts in particular, which in general offer access to a wide range of genres and typical vocabularies. We learn new words and meanings largely through reading; we do not learn words in order to read.

Readability studies

'Readability formulae' are used, though more in the United States than in Britain, to assess the difficulty of published reading material. The procedure with most of them is very simple. Fry (1977), for example, takes word length and sentence length as criteria. In other words, the greater the frequency of long words and sentences in a hundred-word sample, taken from the beginning, middle, and end of a text, the harder the text is judged to be.

Readability formulae look at texts only as products. As Rigg puts it, 'The basic assumption underlying any readability formula is that meaning is in the print, in the text. There is no recognition that meaning is created by each reader as the reader engages with the text' (1986:75).

Even leaving aside issues of social context and individual motivation, and looking at texts as products, the criteria used by readability formulae are doubtful. Factors other than word and sentence length are not accounted for. For instance reduced clauses, which tend to shorten sentences, can create greater difficulty for the reader than longer sentences which are easier to 'unpack'.

Cloze procedure

One approach which focuses on the reader's process through a text rather than on the text itself is cloze procedure. This involves the deletion of words from a passage on a regular basis (for example every fifth word). Readability is assessed through the ease with which the reader is able to provide acceptable items to complete the gapped text.

▶ # TASK 43

In the text below, reproduced later in full in Task 44, every fifth word has been deleted. How readily are you able to choose an acceptable item to complete the text?

It was a beautiful _____ evening. Paul was happy. _____ more exams. College was _____. Now he needed a _____. He wanted to be _____ writer and work for _____ newspaper. But first he _____ a rest.
  It was _____ in the house. There _____ no wind. 'I'll go _____ a walk' said Paul _____ himself. 'I'll go down _____ the river.'
  Paul lived _____ a small town and _____ was soon outside in _____ country. He walked near _____ river and watched the _____ birds.
  Suddenly, he saw _____ girl.

9.4 Simple and simplified texts

While cloze procedure offers us one way of assessing the difficulty of individual texts, we may still need a more comprehensive set of guidelines for selecting a wide range of accessible written material for early readers, that is those who are still coming to grips with some of the ways form, meaning, and function interrelate in written English.

First, can any case be made in principle for simplified texts specially written for a particular group of learners, in this case second language learners? The answer is that it depends on the learners, the circumstances, and the use to which the text is put. And, above all, it depends on the quality of the text.

Many simplified readers designed for second language learners are adaptations of fuller texts, often well-known stories, including classics, by authors such as Dickens or the Brontës. More recent classics have been added to the traditional ones, so that there is now an enormous range of titles to choose from. The best of these do not mechanically follow any readability guides. The advice of Hedge (1988:5), the Editor of 'Oxford Bookworms', to authors who are adapting published novels is: 'It is a good idea . . . to try out an adaptation by creating an intuitive re-telling and then to see what level this fits. You can then work on it further to bring it within the language controls of the most appropriate level.' The result of Hedge's advice is a greater likelihood of producing a narrative where the coherence-creating strategies have arisen naturally from the attempt at simplification and not been imposed in a mechanistic manner.

There are also original narratives specially written, often to publishers' guidelines, for an EFL readership. It was one of these which was selected for the cloze in Task 43 and is given in full in Task 44.

▶ TASK 44

How effective is this as the beginning of a simple narrative? In considering your response, you might draw on the criteria discussed in Task 42, that is the presence of an identifiable genre and the occurrence of exceptional events.

It was a beautiful summer evening. Paul was happy. No more exams. College was finished. Now he needed a job. He wanted to be a writer and work for a newspaper. But first he needed a rest.
    It was hot in the house. There was no wind. 'I'll go for a walk' said Paul to himself. 'I'll go down to the river.'
    Paul lived in a small town and he was soon outside in the country. He walked near the river and watched the water birds.
    Suddenly, he saw the girl.
(*Laird 1978:1*)

The text is written within an identifiable genre: the opening sentence, which leaves date and location unspecified, announces a story genre; the introduction of the girl is presented as a significant event through the simple device of the choice of definite, rather than indefinite, article, indicating that this is a special, unusual girl.

A third category of simple texts belong to genres which are inherently predictable in structure such as fables and folk tales. These genres are characterized by a linear plot and a restricted number of characters, and the story is usually narrated in the simple past tense. Texts in these genres also have the advantage that they have not been written by a single identifiable author. There are numerous equally legitimate versions of 'Little Red Riding Hood' for example, which can range from the extremely simple in theme and structure to the very sophisticated, as we discuss more fully in **11**.

9.5 The notion of authenticity

The use of genres such as folk tales goes some way towards addressing the conflict between the requirements of linguistic simplicity and of authenticity. Because examples of these genres are not identifiable with individual authors, and therefore with single and original versions, any one rendering is equally 'authentic' as long as it stays true to the basic theme, characters, and outcome which are conventionally required of the genre.

The notion of authenticity remains problematic, however. As Meinhof (1987) points out, a strict interpretation of authenticity would include only 'original pieces of written or spoken language which occurred naturally between native speakers and could therefore be accepted as "genuine communicative acts"'. Even if the texts are culled from an authentic source, for example a newspaper, magazine, or novel, where they are clearly doing the job of informing, entertaining, or persuading, there is still the dilemma of texts appearing 'outside their normal socio-cultural environment' (page 40). As soon as texts, whatever their original use, are brought into classrooms for pedagogic purposes they have, arguably, lost authenticity. To address this problem Meinhof suggests a framework in which the learners participate themselves in the collection and selection of texts. The teacher brings in a supply of magazines of all kinds and readerships, and learners choose articles from these. This strategy, of course, is only feasible in cases where this kind of material is readily available.

Authenticity of genre
Many teachers do not have access to a wide range of contemporary 'real-life' material of the kind described by Meinhof and will need to write their own texts or rely on coursebooks which only contain material written for pedagogic purposes. In these cases, while authenticity of writer purpose is arguably lost (that is, the writers are writing primarily as educators), one can attempt to maintain authenticity of genre by allowing the reader to recognize a text as, for example, an advertisement, a ghost story, a love story (see Task 44), and so on. Indeed some teacher-written material is livelier and more interesting than some real-life material.

▶ ## TASK 45

These two extracts are from teacher-written material. How successfully have the writers maintained an authenticity of genre?

Badminton

Badminton is a very popular game. It is a fast game. In the game, people use rackets and a shuttlecock. Players hit the shuttlecock back and forth over a net five feet high. They must return it before it hits the ground. They usually play the game on a court. If there are two players, we call it a singles game. If there are four persons or two pairs of players playing badminton, we call it a doubles game. People can play it both indoors or outdoors. Official tournaments are usually played indoors. But most people play badminton for enjoyment. They usually play it outdoors, like at schools, at offices or at home.

Extract 1 (*Simatupang and Aryanto 1988*)

Some Old-Fashioned Ways of Telling the Time I

In olden days there were no clocks or watches. People told the time by candle or by something called an hour-glass.

The candle clock was very simple, and you can make one for yourself. Buy an ordinary candle. Measure the length of the candle. Note down the correct time from a clock or watch, and then light the candle. Make sure that the candle is not in a draught of air. After 15 minutes blow out the candle. Now measure the candle again and see how much has burnt away. An ordinary candle will burn away at the rate of about a quarter of an inch every fifteen minutes.

Now take the candle and mark off in ¼″ spaces (or whatever the right distance is), like this: You can push small pieces of matchsticks into the side of the candle to mark these distances.

You can use a candle like this for reading a book in the evenings, and it will also tell you the time.

Extract 2 (*Horsburgh 1982:30*)

In the case of extract 1, even though the topic is sport, it is hard to bring to mind a genre category such as 'newspaper sports report', or a description of a process such as 'rules for a game'. In extract 2 the textbook writer shows how it is possible to write a pedagogic text which stays within the generic conventions for a simple set of instructions and, incidentally, maintains a syntactic consistency in the use of the imperative. Genre is a powerful organizing principle and it is helpful, especially for the early second language reader, to be offered texts which follow a clear generic convention and are therefore predictable.

Authenticity of the situation
Widdowson (1979) and Breen (1985) have challenged the notion of authenticity as a feature of texts *per se*. Breen extends the definition of authenticity to encompass all the factors in the teaching situation, including the social context of the classroom and, most importantly, the learner's response to the text. He proposes four types of authenticity:

1 Authenticity of the texts which we may use as input data for our learners
2 Authenticity of the learners' own interpretations of such texts
3 Authenticity of tasks conducive to language learning
4 Authenticity of the actual social situation of the language classroom.
(*Breen 1985:61*)

Breen proposes that teachers ask themselves two questions: (1) Can the learner's own prior knowledge, interest, and curiosity be engaged by this text? (2) In what ways might the learner 'authenticate' the text—i.e. adapt it to his or her own purposes?

Widdowson's view of text authenticity relates to Breen's second question. He proposes that one talk not of texts as having authenticity as things in themselves but, taking a process-oriented view, as being reconstructed on each occasion of their use in line with the reader's purpose. Following this interpretation, a classroom of foreign learners is as legitimate a context for the reconstruction of texts as any other. What is then of interest for the teacher is how he or she can facilitate the interaction between texts and learners. As argued in the conclusion to Section One, the fact that language learners are not usually part of an authentic text's 'model readership' can be a positive advantage if we wish to encourage a more critical, assertive response from the reader.

If we see authenticity as lying in the interaction between text and reader and not in the text itself, we need not hesitate to use specially written texts, and these need not necessarily be written by teachers or textbook writers. Second language learners can benefit from creating their own texts if there is a communicative purpose behind the activity; for example if they are writing stories for another group, or to produce a class diary, or a set of instructions for other students. (We will return to the issue of student-written texts in **11**.)

If we see an authentic reading event as being essentially interactive, this means that readers should be able and willing to critique texts by challenging the kinds of discourses typically embedded in a whole range of genres from advertisements and folk tales to material specially written or adapted for second language learners. In **10** and **11** we look at ways of facilitating this kind of interaction between readers and texts in the classroom.

10 Classroom reading procedures

If we consider that authenticity lies in the interaction of reader with text, rather than merely in features of the text itself, there are several implications. First, as argued in Section One, the reader's interpretation will be supported by various kinds of contextual information. Second language learners need to have available to them information about the immediate, institutional, and wider social context of the text, or at least the opportunity and encouragement to reconstruct it. Secondly, they may be helped by access to the meanings within texts—largely socioculturally determined as argued earlier—in order to draw on relevant kinds of schematic knowledge.

As discussed in **6.4**, there will never be a total coincidence of schemas between writer and reader, even where the writer is targeting a model reader very closely. Nonetheless, there must be some area of agreement about the topic the text is dealing with at least. More disputed territory will be in the area of interpreting *why* a writer describes people as acting or talking in particular ways in texts—the communicative function of the language used. And even more open to interpretation will be the attachment of values to the information or the behaviour described.

10.1 Access to the context of situation

As discussed in **4.1**, in the real world we have access to various kinds of contextual information when we embark on the reading of any text, whether it be a simple 'no parking' sign, a religious tract, or a novel by Charles Dickens. This kind of support for interpretation may be denied the second language learner, especially when confronted with texts included in commercially produced teaching materials.

▶ TASK 46

Consider the opening in this theme-based coursebook to the theme of education. How far is adequate information about the context of the text's production provided for the second language reader?

1 Setting the scene

2 Vocabulary

comprehensive school *n* (l.7) *phr*	school for all children from the age of 11 to 16 or 18
short of *prep phr* (l.11)	not having enough of
PTA *abbrev* (l.15)	Parents and Teachers Association — a group of interested parents and teachers who help the school
high school *n* (l.18)	may now be a comprehensive school, but originally like a grammar school
funds *n* (l.20)	money for a special purpose
lack *vt* (l.25)	not have
grammar school *n* (l.38)	school for academic children, with an entrance exam
maintained school *n* (l.41)	school supported by state money
fees *n* (l.42)	money paid for going to the school
public school *n* (l.44)	private school

3 Text

While you are reading the passage, find the answers to the following questions as briefly as possible:

a) How many different types of secondary school are there in England?

b) What is the biggest problem for the schools today?

c) What are the different ways that people are trying to solve this problem?

■ A CRISIS IN EDUCATION

Bankfield County High School in Cheshire was built in the early sixties, and the buildings have that peculiarly depressed appearance of uncared-for modern architecture that has been allowed to rot and decay. Cheshire has allotted no money for decoration since 1979, so, in the summer of 1985, the new headmaster of Bankfield bought his own paint and paintbrush and tackled his dingy study himself. But even an energetic head cannot maintain an entire comprehensive school. Morale in the school is remarkably high, but Bankfield is being run on the principles of 'muddling through', 'making do': admirable British virtues, but unlikely to prepare future citizens for a high-technology society where only the most skilled will survive.

Bankfield is short of computers, it's short of equipment for physics and electronics (although dedicated teachers, contrary to popular image, have spent

(Brieger and Jackson 1989:31–2)

Although there is a section entitled 'Setting the scene' it is not very informative. We cannot, for instance, very readily relate the two pictures to the headline of the text 'A crisis in education'. Not knowing the author of the text, or the kind of journal in which she is writing (both only named at the end of the article), second language readers may take some time to orientate to the text. First, they are removed from the immediate context in which it was first produced—a perceived 'crisis' in education in 1986—and second, they may not be able to see how particular discourses, about for instance payment for education or educational resources, relate to broader institutional and sociocultural practices.

Other coursebooks include information about the setting of the piece of writing or the author, especially if it is an extract from a longer text such as a novel.

▶ TASK 47

These are two attempts at contextualization which accompany extracts from novels in different advanced level reading coursebooks. Consider how adequate they are.

1 The following extract is from the novel written in 1959. In the extract, Sammy gets to see Beatrice the girl he has fallen in love with.

[*text*]

from 'Free Fall' William Golding 1968
(*Barr, Clegg, and Wallace 1981:17*)

2 The story is set in Nigeria in West Africa at a time when the country was changing very fast. As in many countries, some places, such as the larger cities, were changing more quickly than others. And some people, especially the younger ones, wanted things to change dramatically, while others wanted things to stay as they were.

[*text*]

Chinua Achebe was born in Nigeria and educated at University College, Ibadan. From 1954–1966 he worked for the Nigerian Broadcasting Corporation. He became famous as a writer after the publication of his novels *Things Fall Apart* (1958) and *No Longer at Ease* (1960), both of which are published in many countries. These, like his stories, deal with the problems of Africans living in Africa in the twentieth century.
(*Rossner 1988:56*).

The first is singularly uninformative, merely focusing on the topic and date. The second, apart from being much longer, gives very full information on the setting of the novel. It also presents the extract in the wider context of the writer's work as a whole. Accompanied by a photograph, it is a fair attempt to represent the typical format and language of the blurb which we find on the dust-jackets of novels.

Some textbook writers have taken the issue of textual context even further by looking not just at the context of production but at the context of use. That is, as well as considering the context in which a writer produced a text, one can also consider the context, or likely context, in which a reader will interact with it.

▶ ## TASK 48

How effective is this attempt to place a set of texts in their context of likely use?

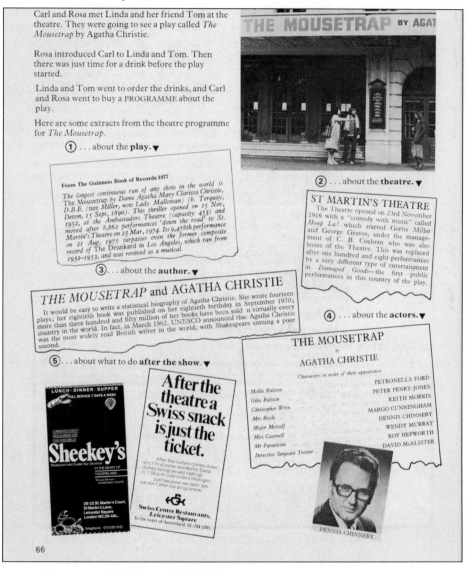

Carl and Rosa met Linda and her friend Tom at the theatre. They were going to see a play called *The Mousetrap* by Agatha Christie.

Rosa introduced Carl to Linda and Tom. Then there was just time for a drink before the play started.

Linda and Tom went to order the drinks, and Carl and Rosa went to buy a PROGRAMME about the play.

Here are some extracts from the theatre programme for *The Mousetrap*.

① . . . about the **play.** ▼

From The Guinness Book of Records 1977

The longest continuous run of any show in the world is The Mousetrap by Dame Agatha Mary Clarissa Christie, D.B.E. (nee Miller, now Lady Mallowan) (b. Torquay, Devon, 15 Sept, 1890). This thriller opened on 25 Nov, 1952, at the Ambassadors Theatre (capacity 453) and moved after 8,862 performances 'down the road' to St. Martin's Theatre on 25 Mar, 1974. Its 9,478th performance on 21 Aug, 1975 surpasses even the former composite record of The Drunkard in Los Angeles, which ran from 1932–1953, and was revived as a musical.

② . . . about the **theatre.** ▼

ST MARTIN'S THEATRE
The Theatre opened on 23rd November 1916 with a "comedy with music" called Houp La! which starred Gertie Millar and George Graves, under the management of C. B. Cochran who was also lessee of the Theatre. This was replaced after one hundred and eight performances by a very different type of entertainment in Damaged Goods—the first public performances in this country of the play.

③ . . . about the **author.** ▼

THE MOUSETRAP and AGATHA CHRISTIE

It would be easy to write a statistical biography of Agatha Christie. She wrote fourteen plays; her eightieth book was published on her eightieth birthday in September 1970; more than three hundred and fifty million of her books have been sold in virtually every country in the world. In fact, in March 1962, UNESCO announced that Agatha Christie was the most widely read British writer in the world, with Shakespeare coming a poor second.

④ . . . about the **actors.** ▼

THE MOUSETRAP
by
AGATHA CHRISTIE

Characters in order of their appearance

Mollie Ralston	PETRONELLA FORD
Giles Ralston	PETER PENRY-JONES
Christopher Wren	KEITH MORRIS
Mrs Boyle	MARGO CUNNINGHAM
Major Metcalf	DENNIS CHINNERY
Miss Casewell	WENDY MURRAY
Mr Paravicini	ROY HEPWORTH
Detective Sergeant Trotter	DAVID McALISTER

DENNIS CHINNERY

⑤ . . . about what to do **after the show.** ▼

LUNCH · DINNER · SUPPER
FULL SERVICE 7 DAYS A WEEK

Sheekey's
Restaurant and Oyster Bar, Seafood
IN THE HEART OF THEATRELAND

28-32 St. Martin's Court,
St Martin's Lane,
Leicester Square
London WC2N 4AL.
Telephone 01-836 4118

After the theatre a Swiss snack is just the ticket.

After the curtain comes down you'll find some wonderful Swiss dishes being served right up to 1.00 a.m. (last orders midnight). Just because we open late we don't alter our programme.

Swiss Centre Restaurants,
Leicester Square
In the heart of theatreland. 01-734 1291.

66

(*Davies and Whitney 1979:66*)

10.2 Access to content

In order to interact effectively with the text, the second language reader needs access to content as well as context. Under the broad heading of content I include genre, topic, and their typical discourses as determined by the institutional and wider social context. Second language readers will need to draw on appropriate schematic knowledge to reach a satisfactory interpretation of the text, though, as argued earlier, this need not mean that such an interpretation will reflect that of either the writer or the model reader. Below I shall consider some ways of helping learners to relate their existing schematic knowledge to the text they are reading.

Pre-reading, while-reading, and post-reading

One way of facilitating a reader's interaction with a text and providing orientation to context and content is, as mentioned in 7.6, through various kinds of text-related tasks. The idea that there are three main types of reading activity, those which precede presentation of the text, those which accompany it, and those which follow it, is now a common feature of discourse about reading (see, for example, Williams 1984; Wallace 1988). Most contemporary reading materials reflect these stages, though in rather different ways.

Pre-reading activities

Some pre-reading activities simply consist of questions to which the reader is required to find the answer from the text. Traditionally this type of question followed the text and was designed to test comprehension, but in more recent materials questions often precede the text and function as scanning tasks—that is the learner reads the text quickly in order to find specific information related to the questions. The three questions in Task 46 are an example of this procedure. One difficulty is that the questions frequently do not seem to be clearly motivated. Why, for example, should the reader read to find the number of different types of secondary school in England, rather than any other kind of information?

Other pre-reading tasks have tended to focus exclusively on preparing the reader for likely linguistic difficulties in a text; more recently attention has shifted to cultural or conceptual difficulties. However, pre-reading activities may not just offer compensation for second language readers' supposed linguistic or sociocultural inadequacies: they may also remind readers of what they do in fact already know and think, that is activate existing schematic knowledge.

▶ TASK 49

Compare these pre-reading activities and consider to what extent they: (1) prepare readers for linguistic features in the following text; (2) prepare readers for conceptual or cultural difficulties, and (3) draw on readers' existing knowledge and views.

d) These words from the story are related to trees. Use them to label the diagrams below.

roots   trunk   branches (or boughs)   leaves
twig   sapling   underbrush (or undergrowth)

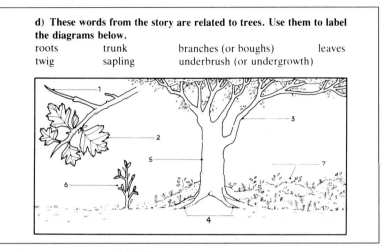

Task A (*Rossner 1988:58*)

1   Before you read the texts, look at the following sentences which are taken from them, and see if you can say whether they were written by the pro-monarchist or the anti-monarchist. In which cases is this clear and in which is it less clear?

  a)   For the Queen, if for nobody and nothing else, masses of ordinary people are anxious and willing to put out flags and throw a national party.

  b)   I believe that the English newspapers have largely failed to register the political significance of the greeting which the ordinary people of Scotland have just given to the Queen and the implications of this for the ultimate unity of the kingdoms.

  c)   In 1977 (the Jubilee has served the function of) covering every intractable problem with excuses for complacent resignation.

  d)   It's all for the tourists really.

  e)   We need a point of unity above and beyond the tensions of everyday public life and controversy . . .

  f)   Thus is the monarch valued, her heritage swallowed by commerce – an attraction worth more than Shakespeare's birthplace and the Soho porn shops rolled into one.

  g)   Today, I think we are in . . . need of our tribal loyalties . . .

  h)   Still, while the tourists take the front seat (to see the Queen), thousands upon thousands of British people are gawping from the galleries.

  i)   There is a natural longing in human beings for legitimacy in government, for an ultimate concept of authority which exists by some kind of legitimate right.

  j)   Such coaches were designed as moving containers of privacy, whose occupants could engage in absorbing discussion, doze or conduct seductions without being observed.

Task B (*Barr, Clegg, and Wallace 1981:106*)

Exercise 2   Wood is a very important natural resource.
a) Which of these purposes is it used for in your country?
- making furniture
- fuel for cooking
- making paper and cardboard
- railway lines
- building houses
- fuel for heating
- making vehicles
- other (what?) _____

b) **Find out where the main forests are in your country and what kinds of trees grow in them.**

c) **Imagine yourself alone in a large forest. Which of the following do you associate with being there?**
- silence
- fear
- other (what?) _____
- noise
- excitement
- darkness
- danger
- light
- peace

Compare your answers with a partner's.

Task C (*Rossner 1988:57*)

Of course many pre-reading tasks aim to do more than just one thing. However task B, written for very advanced learners of English about to tackle a highly culture-specific text, focuses more on 2, while task C focuses on 3. Many pre-reading tasks concern themselves with anticipating language difficulties as does task A. Where language focused pre-reading tasks occur they frequently relate to supposed new vocabulary rather than, for instance, anticipating difficulties with structure.

▶   TASK 50

Compare the pre-reading vocabulary tasks here. Which do you think would be the most effective?

2   Vocabulary

comprehensive school *n* (1.7) *phr*	school for all children from the age of 11 to 16 or 18
short of *prep phr* (1.11)	not having enough of
PTA *abbrev* (1.15)	Parents and Teachers Association — a group of interested parents and teachers who help the school
high school *n* (1.18)	may now be a comprehensive school, but originally like a grammar school
funds *n* (1.20)	money for a special purpose
lack *vt* (1.25)	not have
grammar school *n* (1.38)	school for academic children, with an entrance exam
maintained school *n* (1.41)	school supported by state money
fees *n* (1.42)	money paid for going to the school
public school *n* (1.44)	private school

Task A (*Brieger and Jackson 1989:31*)

Section 3 For Better, For Worse

Part A Marriage

1 Before reading the next texts, look at the words below.
How many of them do you know?
How many of them could you guess? (for example by
splitting the words up: sub - servient; co - habitation)

subservient	strive
impediment	chore
cohabitation	gender
apt	prey
relapse	loot

2 Now look at these words in sentences. It should be easier to guess their meaning.

a) Women, long considered the inferior sex, are therefore expected to be subservient to men.

b) Intolerance can be a serious impediment to successful marriage.

c) Any relationship which involves cohabitation presents problems which are avoided if one lives alone.

d) Married couples behave in predictable ways. For example, they are apt to take on certain roles in the family.

e) In the early days of marriage husbands and wives strive to be on their best behaviour. Later, however, they may relapse into their bad old ways.

f) Gender roles tend to be allocated in marriage. For example, woman are expected to be responsible for cleaning, cooking and other household chores, while men are the breadwinners.

g) The hunter instinct survives in men. Women are still regarded as prey, to be caught and conquered.

h) Traditionally, men bring home the loot in the form of the weekly pay packet.

When you see these words in the text below it should be even
easier to guess their meaning.

Task B (*Barr, Clegg, and Wallace 1981:21–2*)

⊗ Exercise 2 Everybody experiences fear at some time or other, for example when you are woken by a strange noise at night, before you go to the dentist, or when you are on top of a high building. The following words describe different kinds of fear. Using a dictionary if necessary, put the words in the appropriate place on the lines. You may want to put more than one word on a line.

afraid   nervous   terrified   petrified   scared   frightened

A little fear

_____

_____

_____

_____

A lot of fear

Task C (*Rossner 1988:81*)

Task A simply gives a straight gloss of the items as used in the text; task B offers two general strategies to deal with unknown words, first, the etymology of the word itself as discoverable through association with known words; second, the encouragement of the use of context by placing the predicted 'difficult words' in sentences which offer, it is hoped, stronger contextual support than the ensuing text. Task C, by inviting the reader to grade adjectives describing fear, illustrates the particular lexical choices in the following text, the overall theme of which is fear. The author also encourages dictionary use as a pre-reading support. Other writers counsel dictionary consultation as a checking strategy only. Barr, Clegg, and Wallace (1981:10) for instance, advise: 'You can often guess the meaning of a word by looking at how and where it is used. Consult a dictionary ONLY AS A LAST RESORT.'

What both tasks B and C share is a concern not to teach language items related to specific texts but to develop strategies which are employed, in varying ways and to varying degrees, in the reading of all texts. There are two main implications of a strategy-based approach for the design of reading tasks. First, strategies are exercised during the reading of actual texts; we do not 'learn a particular strategy' with a view to then applying it to a text. Second, different strategies are appropriate to different types of text. The overall implications of both these points is that task should match text. For example, we are more likely to reread with care and reflection a favourite poem than a leaflet pushed through the door, and pedagogic tasks can be designed to reflect this variability of response.

If we are to offer our learners a range of genres with varying topics and discourses, it follows that the pre-reading activities aimed to encourage particular reading strategies should vary too.

▶ TASK 51

What kind of text would you expect to accompany these pre-reading tasks?

What do you think?

1   Do you know anyone whom you would describe as an
eccentric? What is it that makes you describe this person in
this way?
The following headings might help you:
   – how they look or dress
   – what their house looks like
   – how they behave to others
   – habits they have
   – opinions or beliefs they hold
   – how they like to spend their time

Task A *(Barr, Clegg, and Wallace 1981:161)*

50 kilos a year

A food that everybody likes – what is it?

- 100 years ago it was very expensive – these days it's cheap and easy to get in most countries.
- In rich countries the average eaten in 1900 was about 8 kilos a year – now it's 50 kilos a year.
- Boys aged 13 to 19 often eat more than 50 kilos a year.
- About 14 *million* African people were taken to the Americas to produce it.

Task B *(Lindop and Fisher 1988:40)*

We might expect the text extract which follows task A to be a descriptive passage in a novel or biography. In fact the passage describes two eccentric elderly ladies and is taken from Laurie Lee's autobiography *Cider with Rosie*. Conversely task B, which presents matters of fact rather than opinion, precedes an informative, factual text about sugar. Thus we see that both content and genre play a part in determining appropriate pre-reading questions. A descriptive, factual text may be preceded by factual questions, possibly in the form of a pre-reading quiz; a discursive text by a task which involves the reader organizing his or her own thoughts about a particular issue, perhaps through a ranking exercise.

Pre-reading questions are sometimes classified in terms of 'fact' or 'opinion'. While this is a broadly useful distinction, it does not allow us to consider a more delicate match between text-type and pre-reading task. The question we should be asking ourselves when we consider pre-reading tasks in the classroom is 'How might the "model" reader approach this text in a real-life situation?' Of course this question immediately raises difficulties, first because, while writers 'position' readers, we must allow the latter the option to be assertive and to read a particular text in a way most congenial to them (see the discussion in **11** below). Second, the classroom is not the same as real life. None the less, as a rule of thumb it is worth thinking about the reasons or range of reasons a reader might read a particular genre in a real-life situation.

One very popular kind of pre-reading task is 'brainstorming'. This may take the form of giving the class a particular key word or key concept, or it may be a newspaper headline or book title. Students are then invited to call out words and concepts they personally associate with the key word or words provided by the teacher. Brainstorming has many advantages as a classroom procedure. First, it requires little teacher preparation; second, it allows learners considerable freedom to bring their own prior knowledge and opinions to bear on a particular issue, and third, it can involve the whole class. No-one need feel threatened when any bid is acceptable and can be added to the framework. For example these are the kinds of associations which might be called up by the key word, 'money': 'coin', 'bank', 'poverty', 'pay day', 'interest', 'purse', 'inflation'. These bids reflect very different categories and levels of generalization. However, the initial random associations can be classified and subcategorized either by the teacher or the students, and additional contributions from class members or the teacher added to 'stretch' existing concepts. The results of this kind of activity resemble what has been called 'semantic mapping', demonstrated in this example of a semantic map for 'language'.

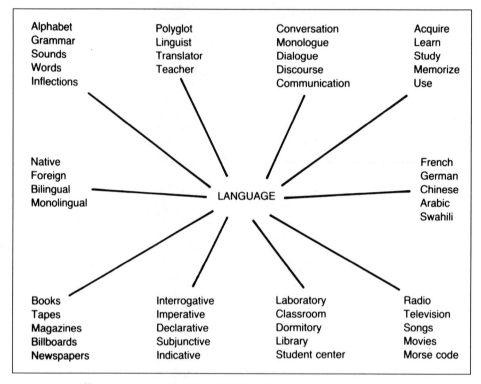

(*Carrell, Devine, and Eskey 1988:247*)

By means of such mapping or brainstorming activities the teacher can guide the class towards the kinds of classifications which will best help them deal with the major concepts contained in the text to be read.

What the reader brings to the reading task determines the strategies he or she is able to use while reading. First, if prior knowledge has been activated by means of a pre-reading task, the reader will be less dependent on the words on the page and will thus be able to minimize the disadvantage of having a less than native speaker proficiency in the language. Second, pre-reading tasks will help the reader to select a strategy appropriate to the reading of that particular text and consistent with reader purpose.

While-reading activities

Generally the aim of while-reading activities is to encourage learners to be flexible, active, and reflective readers (see the discussion in **6.2**). Flexibility is encouraged by inviting the reader to read in ways which are perceived (by the materials writers) to be appropriate to the type of text being presented.

▶ **TASK 52**

How does this pre-reading task invite the reader to read the text which follows it (from a travel brochure) in a particular way?

Unit 7   Holidays in Scotland

Reading for specific information

Suggest hotels for the following people by referring to the information on the opposite page. Sometimes more than one hotel may be suitable; in that case, indicate how much each hotel would cost for a seven-night stay.

1 Two women friends who want to do several all-day hikes in the mountains during the spring.
2 A man with two children aged six and ten, who will spend July in Scotland. The ten-year-old would like to play tennis and the father enjoys squash.
3 A handicapped lawyer who must use a wheelchair but drives her own car. She enjoys concerts, museums, fine architecture and swimming. She will spend the first two weeks of October in Scotland.
4 A writer, a teacher and their one-year-old daughter. They want to be in a quiet place during August. They enjoy good food, and like to take long walks (the baby rides in a back-pack).
5 An older couple, aged 65 and 68. They love mountain scenery and still take easy walks in the mountains when they can. They want to see some of Scotland's famous lochs during May.

(*Walter 1982:36*)

This task is designed to encourage readers to read selectively in line with the particular purpose which the genre 'travel brochure' invites, that is we are likely to approach the text with a set of requirements in mind and scan it to see if those can be fulfilled.

Many while-reading tasks, with the aim of encouraging active and reflective reading, attempt to promote the kind of dialogue between reader and writer which was described in **6**. Different genres offer opportunities for different activities of this kind. For example discursive texts typically present a problem to which there are a number of potential solutions. One can interrupt such texts at points which appear especially to invite a reader contribution. The writer might signal such 'natural breaks' in his or her text in a number of ways, most obviously by means of a question, as in the case of this text taken from *The Female Eunuch* by Germaine Greer:

'Obviously any woman who thinks in the simplest terms of liberating herself to enjoy life and create expression for her own potential cannot accept such a role [i.e. that of a wife]. And yet marriage is based upon this filial relationship of a wife who takes her husband's name, has her tax declared on his return, lives in a house owned by him and goes about in public as his companion wearing his ring on her finger at all times. . . . And yet if a woman is to have children, if humanity is to survive, what alternative can there be?'
(Germaine Greer: *The Female Eunuch*)

A number of possible reader responses can be envisaged at this point, such as 'Well, we could have different kinds of family structure', or 'Don't be ridiculous—children need the conventional family unit', or 'I don't know—you tell me'. Indeed, the question is powerfully predictive of a conclusion to this particular argument which will indeed 'tell' the reader just what those alternatives might be. In fact the reader would feel that the writer had disclaimed responsibility if she did not proceed to do this.

Texts in other genres such as narrative fiction may be divided into sections with intervening questions to encourage learners to predict the continuing events of the story.

▶   TASK 53

How effective is this while-reading task in aiding prediction?

Read the text

Read the first section of the text. Then stop and answer the question. After you have written down your answer, read the next section. If your answer was correct, put a tick (✓) next to it. Do the same with the other sections.

> Baby Carrie was playing on the floor in the sunshine, and suddenly the sunshine was gone.
>   'I do believe it is going to storm[1],' Ma
> 5 said, looking out of the window. Laura looked, too, and great clouds were billowing up[2] in the south, across the sun.

[1]*it is going to storm*: there is going to be a lot of rain and wind
[2]*billowing up*: rising up

1 What do you think is going to happen next? ☐ ——————
Now read on and see if you were right.

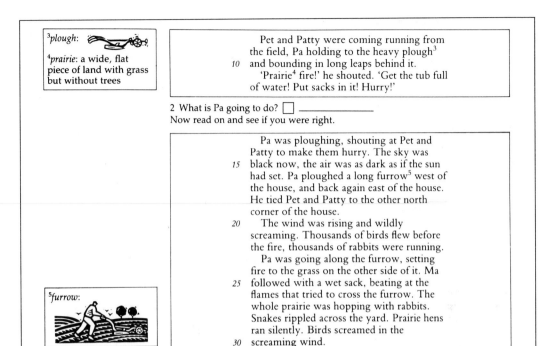

³*plough:*

⁴*prairie*: a wide, flat piece of land with grass but without trees

⁵*furrow:*

Pet and Patty were coming running from the field, Pa holding to the heavy plough³
10   and bounding in long leaps behind it.
'Prairie⁴ fire!' he shouted. 'Get the tub full of water! Put sacks in it! Hurry!'

2 What is Pa going to do? ☐ _____
Now read on and see if you were right.

Pa was ploughing, shouting at Pet and Patty to make them hurry. The sky was
15   black now, the air was as dark as if the sun had set. Pa ploughed a long furrow⁵ west of the house, and back again east of the house. He tied Pet and Patty to the other north corner of the house.
20   The wind was rising and wildly screaming. Thousands of birds flew before the fire, thousands of rabbits were running.
Pa was going along the furrow, setting fire to the grass on the other side of it. Ma
25   followed with a wet sack, beating at the flames that tried to cross the furrow. The whole prairie was hopping with rabbits. Snakes rippled across the yard. Prairie hens ran silently. Birds screamed in the
30   screaming wind.

(*Eckstut and Lubelska 1989:58–9*)

What such activities attempt to do is to replicate the process which occurs quite spontaneously in mature readers where, as noted in **6.1**, we continually use the evidence of what has preceded to predict the continuation of a text. This type of activity is open to criticism for the reason that predicting is largely unconscious in experienced readers. Rossner notes 'there are methodological doubts about it. When does one ever overtly predict the content and meaning of what one is reading or listening to? It happens implicitly' (1988:5). This is undeniably true. However, a feature of many—if not all—classroom tasks is that they make explicit what is, in non-educational settings, implicit.

If one accepts this principle, then there are a range of ways of promoting active engagement with texts as well as interaction between students in the classroom. One suggestion by Davies (1982) is to ask students to locate in the early part of a narrative text a key sentence on which the events of the ensuing story hinge. Another activity, best done in pairs or groups, is to give learners jumbled sentences or sections of text and ask them to reassemble them to form a coherent text. Learners should not just be asked to do the task, but to give their reasons for ordering the sentences or sections in a particular way, thus making it a useful discussion exercise. A similar problem-solving exercise is group cloze, where the cloze procedure is used not to assess text difficulty as in Task 43, but to encourage learners to explore the range of possibilities which the text presents. They draw on their schematic knowledge and knowledge of the language in order to produce a meaningful text. It is not a question of finding a single 'right' answer, but of discussing, and defending if necessary, their choice of item.

One potential problem with group discussion tasks is that quieter or less confident students may contribute nothing. For this reason Doughty and Pica (1986) recommend 'information-gap' tasks, where students require information only possessed by others in order to complete the task. Doughty and Pica's research indicates that there is more interaction when contributions are obligatory. It follows that activities such as jigsaw reading, where each member of a group has one part of a text and individuals must negotiate with other group members to piece together a whole text, tend to produce greater participation.

Other while-reading tasks require students to transfer information from a continuous text to some kind of grid or matrix.

▶ TASK 54

These activities relate to two different kinds of text. Activity A relates to a description of different processes involved in the production of alcoholic drinks, while activity B (overleaf) is based on a physical structure text of the kind described by Johns and Davies (see 8). Which kind of text do you think is better suited to a matrix activity?

Unit 10   Drinks from fruits and grains

Reading for specific information

Complete the following table with information from the passage on the next page. Make sure you check your answers with the text! The column headed *Red wine* is done as an example.

	Red wine	White wine	Beer	Port	Gin	Scotch whisky	Brandy
Made from dark grapes	x						
Made from white grapes							
Made from grain							
Must be drunk quickly	x						
Can be drunk long after it is opened							
Contains no distilled alcohol	x						
Contains some distilled alcohol							
Made completely of distilled alcohol							

Part 3   Processes: How things happen

Early in the development of agriculture men discovered how to make
alcoholic drinks from grapes and corn. The ancient Egyptians drank
both wine and beer, and the Greeks carried on a lively trade in wine
throughout the Mediterranean. The vines of grapes are all of a single
species, *Vitis vinifera*, although there are hundreds of varieties   5
adapted to different soils and climates.
    Wine is the fermented juice of fresh grapes. The juice of the wine
grape contains sugar, and growths of yeast form on the outside of
the grape skins. In wine-making, the grapes are crushed in a wine
press and the yeast converts the sugar to alcohol, when there is no air   10
present, by a process called fermentation. Red wine is made from
dark grapes, and white wine from white grapes or from dark grapes
whose skins have been removed from the wine press at an early stage.
The most famous wine-growing countries are France, Germany and
Italy. Wine was made in England in the Middle Ages, but the climate   15
is not really suitable for grapevines. Wines must be drunk quickly
once they are opened, otherwise bacteria will use the air to convert
the alcohol to vinegar. The bacteria are killed by a higher alcohol
content than is found in wine and that is why sherry and port, the
specialities of Spain and Portugal, are fortified by the addition of   20
spirits to make them last longer.
    Beer is made from sprouting barley grains (malt) which is fer-
mented with yeast to produce alcohol; hops are added for flavour.
Ale, the most common drink in England in the Middle Ages, was also
made from barley, but without hops; the ale of today is merely a   25
type of beer. In Japan beer is made from rice.
    Spirits have a higher alcoholic content than beer and wine and are
made by distillation from a base of grain or some other vegetable.
Gin and vodka can be distilled from a variety of ingredients, including potatoes; gin is flavoured with juniper berries. Scotch whisky is   30
obtained from a base of fermented barley, and brandy from the
distillation of wine. Rum is derived from sugar cane by fermentation
of molasses, a by-product in refining sugar. Cider is made from
apples. South American Indians make alcoholic drinks from cactus
leaves and the shoots of certain palm trees.   35

(From *The Penguin book of the natural world*)

sprouting: beginning to grow.
barley: a grain plant, of the same family as wheat and oats.
hops: seed-cases of a certain flowering plant.
distillation: the process in which a liquid is heated to make a gas, then cooled to make
a liquid again.

Activity A (*Walter 1982:45–6*)

AN EARLY MOTOR CAR (1885)

Benz's first car is now in a museum in Munich. It has one seat and three wheels. There is one small wheel at the front and two large wheels behind the driver's seat. The wheels are made of wood and are surrounded by solid rubber tyres. The chassis is very light and is made of steel tubes.

Between the two back wheels there is a heavy metal flywheel. To the right of the flywheel there is a pulley. A leather belt passes from the pulley to a shaft. The shaft is located under the driver's seat. Metal chains connect the shaft to the back wheels.

Task 14   Complete these tables. Use information from the passage.

TABLE 5

PART	MATERIAL
chassis	
	wood
tyres	
flywheel	
	leather

TABLE 6

PART	LOCATION
the driver's seat	. . . . . . the large wheels
the flywheel	. . . . . . the back wheels
the flywheel	. . . . . . the pulley
the driver's seat	. . . . . . the shaft

Activity B (*Reading and Thinking in English 1980:35*)

Other kinds of while-reading activity may be designed to offer prompts for readers in the case of difficult texts. This was the aim of the design in Task 55.

► TASK 55

This while-reading activity aims to encourage students to take full advantage of the textual context and their own schematic knowledge. How effective is it?

He picked his stick up from his desk and tested it on the air. The first smoker stepped out and
35 raised his right hand. He proffered it slightly *cupped*, thumb tucked into the side, the flesh of the palm ruttled up into soft cushions.
Gryce measured the distance with the tip of his stick, settled his feet, then slowly *flexed* his elbow.
40 When his fist was level with his ear, the hinge flashed open swish down across the boy's palm. The boy blinked and held up his left hand. The stick touched it, curved up and away out of Gryce's peripheral vision, then *blurred* back into it
45 and snapped down across the fingers.
'Right, now get out.'
White-faced, he turned away from Gryce, and *winked* at the others as he passed in front of them to the door.
50 'Next.'
They stepped forward in turn.
They all turned their heads when the door opened and Billy walked into the room.
Mr Farthing, *perched* side-saddle on the edge of
55 the desk, stopped talking and waited for him to approach.
'I've been to see Mr Gryce, Sir.'
'Yes, I know. How many this time?'
'Two.'
60 'Sting?'
'Not bad.'
'Right, sit down then.'
He watched Billy to his place and waited for the class to settle before he continued.
65 'Right *4C*. To continue.'

from *Kes* by Barry Hine, 1968

What shape does this suggest?

What do you do with your elbow to bring your fist level with your ear?

How fast is the cane moving?

What kind of signal must a 'wink' be? Why does he do it?

Think about the teacher's likely position.

4C is obviously part of a numbering system, but what could it refer to here?

(*Barr, Clegg, and Wallace 1981:82*)

The idea was to encourage the reader not to 'guess the missing word' but to see how its general content area could be guessed from the surrounding context. A variation on this is to use multiple choice items not to test but to teach and guide, to encourage the reader to use the available clues in the ongoing text, and to see how meaning accumulates throughout the text.

▶ TASK 56

How far is the reader able to 'accumulate meaning' as he or she progresses through the text below?

To get there at all you have a long drive over mountain roads, and after you leave your car at the "no vehicle traffic" sign you
10 have a fairly long rough walk to find the hidden valley where the tepees cluster on each side of a stream.

The tribe, as they call themselves, are gradually buying up the land on which their tepees sit but the farmer — who bought his
15 land at £10 an acre has upped his price recently to nearly £700 which makes it very difficult.

20 Each person coming in passes a kind of entrance test, building tepee. Carol, mother of four children, ranging from eight to fourteen, said: "I met a couple of people from the tepee village and they asked me to come. I said I would be there in a fortnight – but I uprooted and went straight away. My
25 great grandparents were American Indians so I suppose I just felt at home. It took me a fortnight to make the tent. The village has a big old heavy duty treadle sewing machine you can use."

b) *tepee* is likely to mean:
   i) a kind of animal
   ii) a tree
   iii) a type of accommodation
   iv) a person

c) *tepee* is likely to mean:
   i) a camping tent
   ii) an American Indian tent
   iii) a commercially produced tent
   iv) a circus tent

(Barr, Clegg, and Wallace 1981:10–11)

A major problem with while-reading tasks of this kind is that they can be very time-consuming to prepare. Another objection is that they are not 'natural', interrupting the reading flow. Again one might respond—as to the objection about prediction tasks—that the aim is to make explicit what for the skilled reader would be implicit. This type of task can help readers in classroom situations to be more aware of the reading process and what is involved in it, as well as their own reading strategies.

Post-reading activities
Traditionally the major, often only, kind of post-reading activity consisted of questions which followed a text. Indeed, many coursebooks still adopt this well-tried formula. Multiple choice questions can frequently be answered without reference to the text at all—that is the reader need only draw on existing schematic knowledge.

▶ TASK 57

How far is it possible to answer these questions without referring to the text to which they relate?

Mary's husband Lord Darnley had been

a) killed in the explosion at Kirk O'Field
b) told to wake up all the people of Edinburgh
c) startled by the explosion at Kirk O'Field
d) stabbed by the people of Edinburgh
(Gill 1969:22)

We can probably agree that options (b) and (d) can be pretty well ruled out on the grounds that it is hard to imagine circumstances in which one would wake up the whole population of a big city or in turn be stabbed by such a large number. Option (c) can be discounted on the grounds of triviality; to indicate that someone was startled by an explosion is surely hardly worth saying. Moreover, with traditional post-reading questions of this kind it is almost always a case of providing 'right' or 'wrong' responses. There is not usually allowance for a continuum of 'least' to 'most satisfactory' interpretations, with the quality of the defence of the interpretation counting as a major consideration in evaluating the adequacy of the response.

There is a place for post-reading tasks but, as with pre- and while-reading tasks, the activity needs to be motivated by the genre, the context of learning, and likely learner purpose. Some texts naturally lend themselves to follow-up writing tasks. For example, a natural response to the reading of 'The blame that Spain must share' (page 16) for my class, who were studying English in Britain at the time, was to write to the Editor of the newspaper, expressing our shared views.

Other texts might lend themselves to follow-up activities such as role-play.

▶ **TASK 58**

Consider how this text could be used for role-play in the language classroom.

Choosing between the systems

We wonder whether you can give us some educational advice regarding our daughter, Penelope, aged nine. At present she is in the third year at the local county junior school. In her first year she was in the top five per cent; in her second year she was in the top ten per cent. At present she seems to be doing well and enjoys school, although the staff do not appear to be stretching her and this year no homework is given out. However we are concerned about her prospects when she moves in two years' time to the comprehensive secondary school in the neighbourhood. This school has only just become fully comprehensive, and we are disturbed by reports of poor standards of academic achievement (little importance seems to be given to formal exams at CSE or O level) and poor discipline. One of Penelope's teachers has advised us that she should do better in a more academic setting.

We are therefore contemplating sending Penelope to a private prep school in the district. This school takes children from seven to 13 years of age. Starting at the age of 10, Penelope would be just in time to start the school's science course, and also Latin. She would unfortunately have missed two years' French, and would find it hard work to catch up on this. The problem really is that we shall find it hard to afford the cost of this schooling and we do not expect to be able to follow up three years' schooling at the prep school with continued higher costs at a private boarding school, unless Penelope is fortunate to win a scholarship to one. There is no private day school in this area. It is therefore likely that Penelope will have to return to state comprehensive schooling at the age of 13.

Do you think that three years' private schooling is worth it, in view of the 'jolt' to the child on returning to a state comprehensive. This raises the problems of mixing with a less disciplined group, finding that some of the interesting studies she was undertaking are either dropped completely or tackled at a much lower level and finding some subjects taught in a different way. We recognise of course that she would be given a tremendous 'boost' by the period of private schooling, with a pupil/teacher ratio of up to 18 to one, and would have the opportunity of competing for a scholarship at 13.

(Barr, Clegg, and Wallace 1981:41)

A colleague of mine exploited this text by designing a role-play activity involving Penelope, her parents, and various neighbours, each of whom presented their opinion regarding Penelope's education.

In **10** we have emphasized that reading activities can promote an interaction between reader and text which is, in Widdowson's terms, 'authentic'. A guiding principle in designing activities as coursebook writers or planning them as classroom teachers is to encourage an engagement with the text which is appropriate to its genre and content, the context of situation, and, above all, the learners' purposes in reading it. So far, however, we have assumed rather conventional and typical responses to texts on the part of a model reader. In **11** we will look at approaches which encourage a more critical approach to second language reading in terms both of text selection and classroom procedure.

11 Texts and classroom procedures for critical reading

This unit develops the discussion presented in **9** and **10** on text selection and the treatment of texts in the classroom. It aims to take a closer look, first at the cultural values implied in the selection of texts by teachers or coursebook designers, and second, at ways in which we might encourage more critical responses to written texts in the classroom. As noted in **6**, the second language reader may be disadvantaged in interaction with a text in a foreign language, not so much because of inadequate linguistic or schematic knowledge but because of an over-deferential stance towards the text. We might therefore wish to make the interaction with the text a more equal one for the second language reader by drawing attention to the range of different possible ways of approaching, interpreting, and evaluating texts. In doing so, we can build on the pre-, while-, and post-reading procedures described in **10**.

In **11** we will consider approaches to text selection and task design which:

1 Encourage learners to be alert to the culture-specific content of texts and tasks and, where possible, active in their own selection or production of texts and tasks.

2 Encourage learners to be more aware of their own strategies and roles as readers and how these are socioculturally influenced.

3 Offer learners critical reading strategies which allow them to critique the discourses within texts, that is, to challenge taken-for-granted ways of talking about people, places, and events in order to allow alternative readings to emerge.

11.1 Critical approaches to text selection

Problem-posing: Freirean approaches

One approach is to select texts for their potential to raise issues. This approach involves considering texts as 'codes' in the sense that they encode issues which pose problems for a particular group of learners. The role of the student is then to identify the problems which may lie within the genre, topic, or the discourses embedded in the text. In other words, it is not a question of *solving* the problems set by the teacher or coursebook writer but of perceiving what are problematic issues arising from a text.

These may relate to the learner's situation as a member, for instance, of a cultural or linguistic minority, or they may have more global significance.

This problem-posing approach originated with the work of Paulo Freire (see, for example, Freire 1976) who in the 1950s initiated a literacy programme for Brazilian peasants which took as its starting point the issues, identified by the learners themselves, which closely affected the lives of this disempowered group of people. Freire's view was that literacy was one route to empowerment, involving an externalizing—and therefore greater critical awareness—of people's place in the wider society.

In the teaching situation, the Freirean approach has used pictures designed to reflect the social circumstances of the learners and to trigger key words which have a resonance for them, for example *'favela'* ('slum') and *'governo'* ('government'). Pictures are often used in the second and foreign language classroom as cues for language and literacy work, for example to draw out conceptual or affective responses for general discussion purposes, or as a pre-reading activity. However, there is no reason why they should not also be used to generate more critical responses of a sociopolitical kind—that is to raise problems rather than attempt to solve them, to question rather than to react.

▶ TASK 59

This is a visual pre-reading task which precedes a short story by the American writer Ray Bradbury included in Rossner (1988). Rossner uses the pictures to encourage students to make a conceptual link and thus anticipate the development of the story. To what extent could the two pictures also be used to pose a problem?

Exercise 4   Look at the two pictures. With a partner invent a story in which they could be related.

(Rossner 1988:96)

Pairs of pictures of this kind can be used not just to arouse feelings, or to indicate some conceptual link which will be developed in the story. They can also be used to present a dilemma, a paradox, through the juxtaposition of images, in this case of peace and violence, or—as one of my students put it—of construction versus destruction.

Auerbach and Wallerstein (1987) take a problem-posing approach in a book entitled *ESL for Action: Problem Posing at Work*. As well as visuals, they use as codes simple texts, usually dialogues but also narratives, which are calculated to encourage students to identify with the issues and problems presented. The idea is that students are free to make what interpretation they wish from the text. At the same time the hope is clearly that the text will act as a trigger to lead students to draw on personally and socially relevant experiences in discussing what they perceive as problematic in the situation presented.

▶ TASK 60

Here is a typical code from Auerbach and Wallerstein. Could you use this or similar material with your own group of students?

(*Auerbach and Wallerstein 1987:25*)

One criticism is that this approach is manipulative. It assumes that learners wish to explore in public what may be personal and painful issues. One answer to this objection is that they do not need to. The fictional element in this kind of material allows discussion to proceed at a safe distance from 'real life'. Of course it is not just fictitious case studies which can act as codes. Well-chosen true-life stories, from a newspaper for instance, can serve a similar purpose. The important thing is to select texts which are accessible, but rich enough to offer learners choice in their manner of interpretation so that they do not feel there is clear 'right' or 'wrong' response.

Very often issues—simply because they are politically or socially sensitive—cannot easily be addressed in the home language and context of the learners. A second or foreign language context can provide enough distance from the same, or related, issues to allow students to make the connections they wish.

In a problem-posing approach, the students can themselves provide input for the code. They can be invited to bring into class different kinds of documents, including visuals, or texts with visual support such as advertisements, which function for them, in one way or another, as codes.

Literature texts as codes
Auerbach and Wallerstein's book is concerned with job-related literacy and their texts tend consequently to be chosen from a restricted range of genres and topics. However an obvious source of material for a code-based approach is literature. Literary texts may well, in part at least, encode students' own experiences and give rise to strong or varied responses.

Literature may also be produced by learners themselves as part of what is known as a 'language experience' approach. One technique used in this approach, especially with early learners, involves the students providing an oral narrative of a personal experience, or composing an oral text such as a poem or a story. The student him- or herself, or the teacher acting as scribe, may then produce a written version. This, in turn, may be edited and redrafted as a polished version to be read by other groups of students. Much language experience material not only encodes very personal and private experiences, but sets them in a wider social context and may therefore echo the experiences of quite different groups of learners and motivate them to produce their own language experience material.

▶ TASK 61

This poem is part of a collection produced by learners in Zimbabwe. What kinds of integrated language activity, for example discussion or writing tasks, might emerge from it if presented in: (1) the learners' own context? (2) Your own classroom context?

Give me a meaningful name
Priscilla Dube

They call me Priscilla.
What strange, weighty armour
To put on an African child.

Priscilla is no more than a lifetime burden.
To my grandparents it symbolises nothing
It is a curse on my ancestral spirits.

You call me by the name of a saint
But my ancestors
Who died for just causes
Are they all in the flames of hell?

When will we have
A Saint Lobengula or Saint Kagubi?
Does God close the gates of Heaven
To African history-makers?

Let some call me Priscilla,
But you, my brothers,
Gathered in front of the tombs of our ancestors,
When the horn of sacrifice sounds,
Give me a meaningful name.

I shall answer happily,
Tears of joy in my eyes,
My soul will be satisfied.
Blood will flow through my veins
Like the water of a flooded river.

I will then take off the old mantle,
Be she a saint or a martyr,
And put on the gown of my ancestor,
Be she a heroine or a rain-maker.

(*Zimbabwe School Readers Series: 'Young Voices': 1986*)

The text is likely to function as a code for many second language students who have settled in, or who are visitors to, English-speaking countries, as well as those in post-colonial situations who have felt obliged to change or adapt their names for a range of reasons.

Cross-cultural material

Texts are necessarily culturally loaded. In reading any authentic text one is 'reading the culture' of the original writer and readers of that text. As noted in Section One, highly culture-specific content can create difficulties for foreign and second language learners. An approach which turns this potential problem to positive advantage is represented by the material in

Task 62. This is taken from a book prepared in the People's Republic of China by a team of Chinese and British teachers. Its overall theme is 'cross-cultural life-styles and attitudes'. So, for example, it is suggested that compliments and congratulations are more readily offered in some situations in Western cultures than in China.

▶ ## TASK 62

This set of texts was designed to highlight some cultural differences between China and Britain.

1 Could you use these or similar texts in your own teaching situation?

2 Can you see any problems in using such texts?

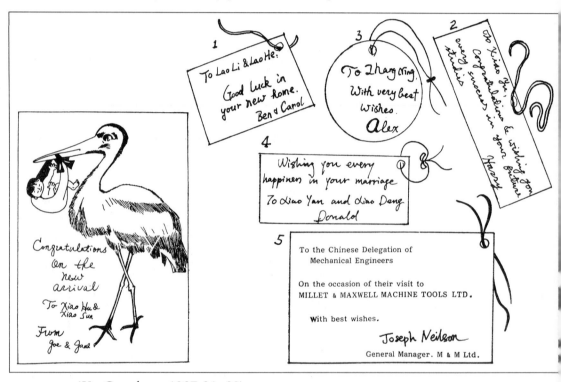

(*Xu Guozhang 1987:81, 83*)

One principle behind such material is that students can move from the known to the unknown. The physical setting is Chinese but the situations presented are cross-cultural, that is occasions when people from the West are in social or professional contact with Chinese people. While the idea seems to be that the Chinese should be sensitive to Western customs even in their own country, and there is little suggestion that Western visitors might adapt to Chinese customs, the way is nonetheless open for particular cultural practices, and the values and beliefs attached to them, to be directly addressed. In other words, cross-cultural difference becomes the topic itself.

Texts which offer alternative discourses

One danger with materials which take distinctive cultural practices as their content, like the stork card in Task 62, is that life-styles and attitudes tend to be stereotyped. After all, not all British people send commercially produced cards to the parents of a new-born child. We can therefore offer students texts which show how different writers, even when dealing with the same general topic, can draw on different genres and discourses. One recent publication which aims to illustrate this is entitled *Contrasts* by David Foll (1990). In each unit the book presents two texts dealing with the same topic but from different genres, or of the same genre and topic but presenting different sets of discourses. So, for example, the topic of 'youth training' is presented respectively in a Government information leaflet and a newspaper article, while the language of politics is presented in two political manifestos, written by each of the major political parties in Britain.

▶ TASK 63

Here, and on page 110, are two texts used in *Contrasts*. They were selected to draw attention to 'the content, language and style of two opposing political manifestos'. Could you use similarly contrasting texts in your own teaching context? If so, how would you use them?

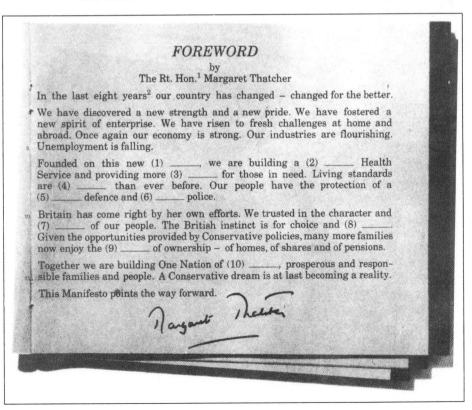

FOREWORD
by
The Rt. Hon.[1] Margaret Thatcher

In the last eight years[2] our country has changed – changed for the better.

We have discovered a new strength and a new pride. We have fostered a new spirit of enterprise. We have risen to fresh challenges at home and abroad. Once again our economy is strong. Our industries are flourishing. Unemployment is falling.

Founded on this new (1) _____, we are building a (2) _____ Health Service and providing more (3) _____ for those in need. Living standards are (4) _____ than ever before. Our people have the protection of a (5) _____ defence and (6) _____ police.

Britain has come right by her own efforts. We trusted in the character and (7) _____ of our people. The British instinct is for choice and (8) _____. Given the opportunities provided by Conservative policies, many more families now enjoy the (9) _____ of ownership – of homes, of shares and of pensions.

Together we are building One Nation of (10) _____, prosperous and responsible families and people. A Conservative dream is at last becoming a reality.

This Manifesto points the way forward.

INTRODUCTION BY THE LEADER OF THE LABOUR PARTY

Every election is a time of decision. But this General Election on June 11[1] faces the British people with choices more sharp than at any time in the past fifty years.

The choices are between Labour's programme of work for people and Tory[2] policies of waste of people: between investment in industrial strength, and acceptance of industrial decline; between a Britain with competitive, modern industries, and a Britain with a low tech, low paid, low security economy increasingly dependent upon imports.

The election will decide whether we and our children are to live in a country that builds high standards of care for all who need treatment for (1) _____, pensions in retirement, good grounding in education, fair chances to get on; or in a country where the Conservatives go on running down the vital health, education and (2) _____ services of every community, imposing higher (3) _____ and lower (4) _____.

This election will decide whether our country is to be a United Kingdom or a (5) _____ kingdom; one that is brought together by proper division, prudent investment and concern for the (6) _____ of the whole nation, or one that is pulled apart by (7) _____, cuts, increased privilege for the richest and (8) _____ for the rest.

This election will decide whether we put our resources into the real defence provided by a modern, (9) _____ army, navy and airforce safeguarding our country and supporting NATO[3]; or spend those sums on maintaining an ageing system of nuclear weapons, while buying a new generation of missiles which cannot give our country effective (10) _____. It will decide whether Britain is part of the international process of nuclear build-down or ruled by a government uniquely intent upon nuclear build-up . . .

(*Foll 1990:33, 34*)

(With each text the students are told to 'work with your partner to fill each gap with one or two possibilities that make sense in the context'.)

Contrasts is designed on the principle that one way in which we build up schemas is through access to a wide variety of texts with varying discourses. We can thus see how the description of persons, places, or phenomena will be embedded in different kinds of discourses depending on the writer's view of the institutions to which they relate, and the genre the writer is working within.

One can also show how discourses can vary by collecting examples of different ways of writing—not about the same institution or social behaviour—but the same event. The text 'The blame that Spain must share' (page 16), for instance, can be seen in the context of news reports of similar events, or series of events, over the summer of 1989. In this way the existence of different ways of writing about the same event can be highlighted. And where there has been international coverage of an issue or event, students can read texts which have appeared in their own newspapers for comparison.

11.2 Heightening learners' awareness of their strategies and roles as readers

As well as thinking critically about text selection, we can encourage in learners a greater awareness of themselves as readers. In **11.2** we will consider ways in which readers might reflect critically on their role when interacting with foreign language texts.

Awareness of individual learning strategies

There has lately been considerable interest in heightening learners' general awareness, not just of what texts can offer them but of their own learning processes. One part of this is their awareness of their behaviour as readers. This was discussed in **7.4** in terms of metacognitive strategies—the awareness of one's own thinking and learning strategies. A process approach is strongly associated with the principle of metacognition and can be exploited in the classroom in various ways, some of which we discussed in **10**, for instance encouraging learners to predict the continuation of a text while articulating the linguistic and schematic resources on which they draw. However the metacognitive approach has tended to focus on thinking and learning behaviour in an individualistic way. We might encourage learners to be aware not only of their own possibly idiosyncratic behaviour, as readers but of ways they have been socialized into certain patterns of reading behaviour, and ways they are addressed not as individuals but as members of a social group such as 'students' or 'consumers' or 'foreigners'. In short, as well as awareness of individual cognitive processes we need to be aware of reading as a social process.

Awareness of the social role of the reader

One sense in which the reader's role is social as much as individual is that readers are addressed, usually implicitly, as members of social groups determined by, for example, gender, class, or nationality. Textbook writers can present texts, as argued earlier in **11.1**, so as to deliberately draw attention to their cultural loading. However some coursebooks continue to present highly culture-specific material as unproblematic, making assumptions about shared knowledge of life-styles and values from which significant groups of second language readers are likely to be excluded, for example texts about events or phenomena such as dinner parties, dieting, and dating. One way of using these texts for critical reading in the classroom is to encourage the reader to explore the ways in which a specific readership is written into the text. This may be revealed not only through what is stated in the text but what is omitted.

▶ ## TASK 64

This is a text from a course in reading for academic purposes. How do the text and the pre-reading questions prescribe a model reader for this text?

Part 2
Expressing past time

The passage is about an explorer of the 16th century. This map shows where he went. Read the passage and answer these questions: *a What was the achievement of Magellan? b What was the achievement of the men who returned to Spain?*

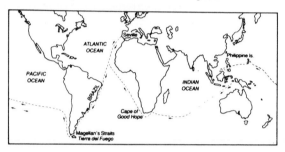

Early in the 16th century men were trying to reach Asia by travelling west from Europe. In order to find Asia they had to find a way past South America. The man who eventually found the way from the Atlantic Ocean to the Pacific was Ferdinand Magellan.

Magellan sailed from Seville in August 1519 with five ships and about 280 men. Fourteen months later, after spending the severe winter on the coast of Patagonia, he discovered the channel which is now called Magellan's Straits. In November 1520, after many months of dangers from rocks and storms, the three remaining ships entered the ocean on the other side of South America.

They then continued, hoping to reach Asia. But they did not see any land until they reached the islands off the coast of Asia. Before they arrived at these islands, later known as the Philippines, men were dying of starvation. While they were staying in the Philippines, Magellan was killed in battle. The remaining officers then had to get back to Spain. They decided to sail round Africa. After many difficulties, one ship with eighteen men sailed into Seville three years after leaving. They were all that remained of Magellan's expedition. However, their achievement was great. They were the first men to sail round the world.

(Reading and Thinking in English 1979:53)

Some students of mine from South East Asia observed that the text is written solely from a European point of view, that of the explorers rather than the peoples of the lands which they—visited—explored—colonized? Of course it can be objected that the text is about exploration; it is not the author's intention to tackle the complex topic of exploitation. An awareness of the restricted perspective of the writer, however, allows one to use such a text in the classroom by, for example, asking students to rewrite the text from the point of view of some of the 'invisible' participants, such as the people of the Philippines.

Moreover, the questions which precede the text also position the reader. Indeed, one can argue that pre-reading questions or tasks of whatever kind impose on learners a way of reading the text. This is one of the problems with the tasks illustrated in **10** and lends support to the value of learner-generated tasks as noted in **11.3**. And tasks as well as texts can be culturally insensitive in the kinds of assumptions they make about the model reader.

▶ # TASK 65

Would this pre-reading task which precedes an extract from *The Color Purple* by Alice Walker present any difficulties to your own students? If not, can you imagine what difficulties it might present to some groups of students?

Preparation

Task 1

> **This activity will help you to clarify your own ideas of what a 'sexist husband' is.**

1   There are many differing views on what the ideal relationship between a husband and wife is. Which of the following views do you support?

  ☐   a   The role of the wife should be that of caring for the husband, the children and the house; the role of the husband should be to provide for the family.

  ☐   b   The role of the wife and that of the husband should be discussed until there is mutual agreement about what they should be.

  ☐   c   There should be no role-typing: both husband and wife should be prepared to undertake any task related to the marriage.

2   What do you think are the typical features of a 'sexist husband'? Make a list. Compare your list with that of other students in your group.

(*Tomlinson and Ellis 1988:12*)

The extract in Task 65 carries the assumption that attitudes to sexism are entirely personal, whereas discourses which assume a range of options in the sexual and marital roles we take on, as those of this extract do, may not be available to students in some cultural contexts.

We see then that it is not just texts but tasks which can position the reader. Indeed, in using such materials a teacher might wish to encourage critical awareness of the task as well as the text on the principle that a complete pedagogic text includes the accompanying questions and suggested activities. This brings us to the third aspect of a critical reading approach, the development of a classroom procedure which encourages students to challenge certain features of both texts and tasks.

11.3 A critical reading procedure

We might draw on the framework offered by Kress (1985:7) (see **2.2**) in which he raises three questions as a starting point for critical reading:

1 Why is this topic being written about?
2 How is this topic being written about?
3 What other ways of writing about the topic are there?

These can be related to the three phases, pre-reading, while-reading, and post-reading described in **10**. Thus a pre-reading question might, rather than ask the reader to anticipate the particular writer's treatment of a topic, invite him or her to consider why the topic has been selected at all. Kress's second question will relate to the while-reading phase in terms, for example, of scrutinizing the writer's linguistic choices in order to find support for the existence of a certain point of view. In the post-reading phase students can consider how the text *might have been* written, for example by another writer in another context for a different model reader. Below we will look at some pre-, while-, and post-reading activities which take a critical perspective.

Pre-reading activities

Students provide their own questions, statements, or hypotheses   Students can be encouraged to raise their own questions about texts rather than answering given questions which dictate a way of reading the text. This is similar to a well-established procedure known as 'SQ3R' (Survey, Question, Read, Recite, Review) first propounded by F. P. Robinson in 1946, where the reader undertakes a preliminary survey which raises questions he or she expects the text to answer. One difference with a more critical approach is that the aim is not solely to find answers but to raise further questions in the course of reading. They may in turn motivate the reading of further texts dealing with similar issues. Alternatively, students can be asked to generate not questions but statements, to be supported or denied by a reading of the text. Some students may have considerable knowledge of the topic dealt with by the text. They can organize this existing knowledge in the form of statements such as 'less than five per cent of British Members of Parliament are women' which can be verified or falsified by the other students during the subsequent reading of the text. Alternatively, students can state their own opinions as the basis of a pre-reading 'agree/disagree' task rather than do ready-made pre-reading tasks like those described in **10**.

One can focus this activity a little more by encouraging the students to hypothesize about ways in which the topic of the text might be dealt with. In doing so, Kress's third question can be adapted: 'What ways are there of writing about the topic?' Such a question could, for example, replace the pre-reading questions provided by the coursebook writers in the case of the 'Magellan' text in Task 64. Thus, the students might simply be given the word 'Magellan' and, before looking at the text at all, be asked to respond to the question 'What could the writer choose to write about?' Answers might include:

- the different races, or language groups, encountered by Magellan during his voyage
- how communication was achieved with the people encountered
- the effect on people of Magellan's landing on their territory
- the health and well-being of Magellan and his crew

This activity helps to highlight the particular discourse selections actually made by the writer. An appropriate post-reading question would then be 'What options regarding an approach to the topic were/were not taken up by the writer?'

Cross-cultural pre-reading tasks   One option in the case of highly culture-specific texts is to design cross-cultural pre-reading tasks which invite comparison between features of the students' own culture and the target culture. This kind of activity is particularly suitable for use with advanced students.

▶ TASK 66

Consider how far this pre-reading task encourages the reader to compare phenomena related to social class in his or her own culture with those which relate to the British context.

What do you think?

How do people judge social class in your country? Put the following factors in order of importance, adding any other factors you consider important.

- how much you earn
- what job you do
- how you speak
- how you think
- how well-mannered you are

- how well-educated you are
- who your parents are
- how you dress
- where you live

(*Barr, Clegg, and Wallace 1981:68*)

Pre-reading tasks which challenge conventional outcomes   Some teaching materials, such as the example in Task 67, present story texts with what we might call deviant discourses, in which some of the conventions of the genre are changed. For instance in one fairy story the princess rescues the prince rather than vice versa, and in 'Little Red Riding Hood' it is Grandmother and Little Red Riding Hood, rather than the hunter, who kill the wolf. The students are asked to do pre-reading tasks which encourage them to draw on their schemas for the genre.

▶   TASK 67

How effectively does the pre-reading task opposite invite students to explore conventional views of heroes and heroines?

The reader is then introduced to the stories of Mizilca and Philbert respectively, who each break all the rules laid down for conventional heroines and heroes. One advantage of this kind of activity is that classroom discussion can take place at an elementary or quite a sophisticated level. Students can also participate in making up their own deviant fairy or folk tales, along the lines of a recent children's story called 'Sleeping Ugly'!

While-reading activities

Offering students alternative readings of a text   It is possible to devise tasks which offer the reader the possibility of more than one way of reading a text. The authors of a collection entitled *Reading Stories* (Mellor, O'Neill, and Patterson 1987) look in particular at the kind of disparity of values which may exist between a writer writing in the past and a contemporary reader. A late twentieth-century reader has a different set of socially-determined responses to call upon from that of a reader of even ten or twenty years ago. For this reason, discourses drawn upon by ELT materials writers writing even in the late seventies or early eighties may be challenged by contemporary readers. With many second language readers there is yet another dimension as the reader is reading not just at a distance of time but from a different cultural perspective.

Mizilca & Philbert

BEFORE READING

You are going to read two stories. One has a young heroine (woman) called Mizilca; the other has a young hero (man) called Philbert.

From your knowledge of typical fairy stories or folk tales what would you expect **Mizilca** (the heroine) and **Philbert** (the hero) are going to be like?

Write the sentences that you would expect to be true of Mizilca and Philbert, if they were the usual kind of heroine and hero, on to your copy of the chart under the heading EXPECTATIONS.
(You'll fill in the other columns after you have read the stories.)

— to be weak and afraid

— to be a fearless knight

— to like adventures

— to be able to fight fiercely

— to like beautiful silk materials and jewels

— to like to stay at home quietly

— to enjoy excitement and action

— to look beautiful

— to think personal appearance is very important

— to fight battles

CHARACTERS	Mizilca	Philbert
EXPECTATIONS What we expect the characters to be like:		
BEHAVIOUR What the characters are like in the stories:		
QUALITIES What qualities the characters show:		

(Mellor, Hemming, and Legget 1984:16)

▶   TASK 68

What do you think is the aim of this while-reading task which accompanies a story entitled 'The Whole Town's Sleeping' by Ray Bradbury; It is a suspense story describing a woman's probable rape and murder.

During reading

1.   Think about the arguments put forward by different readers of this story and to what extent you agree or disagree with their readings.

The arguments are summarised below. It may be possible to begin recording your agreement or disagreement as you read.

Two readings: a comparison		
Reading 1: 'a clever, entertaining suspense story'	**Agree**	**Disagree**
1. Has an engrossing plot.		
2. Is a cleverly constructed story.		
3. Has deft and amusing characterisation.		
4. Skilfully evokes the heroine's fear.		
5. Encourages a reading of violence as entertaining.		
Reading 2: 'unacceptable, offensive..'		
1. Accepts and confirms as 'natural' that most violent attacks on women are by men.		
2. Accepts and confirms that women may be victims of violence because of what they are - women.		
3. Implies women are silly to go out alone.		
4. Implies women who are victims of violence are to blame in some way.		
5. Encourages a reading of violence as entertaining.		

(Mellor, O'Neill, and Patterson 1987:70)

The writers of this task note 'a few years ago "The Whole Town's Sleeping" was read solely as an exciting suspense story. Recently however there has been criticism of the story and the assumptions it expects readers to share' (Mellor, O'Neill, and Patterson 1987:70). The reading task in Task 68 aims to highlight the viability of different interpretations on the part of a contemporary reader.

Identifying parallel discourses   One can identify parallel discourses in some texts, for instance where contrasting people, places, countries, or phenomena are described. It then becomes interesting to examine how these contrasting discourses unfold in the course of a text, frequently signalling a differential treatment of participants. That is, the writer's use of language favours one person or social group over another, often in ways that are not immediately apparent.

► TASK 69

Look again at the text 'The blame that Spain must share' (page 16). Can you see an approach to the analysis of this text which would help to highlight for learners the author's contrasting treatment of Spain and the Spanish and Britain and the British, the latter represented by the figure of Robbie?

One idea is to ask the students to make two lists headed respectively 'the Spanish' and 'Robbie'. Under each heading learners might put predicates (noun or verb phrases, or adjectives) which are associated with each participant. What emerges is two sets of lexical 'chains' which look like this:

The Spanish	*Robbie*
exploitation	not really a lager lout
pour alcohol	lives . . . in a sleepy market town
turned a . . . problem into a disaster	neat
factory for lager louts	quiet
nurtured	supporter of his cricket club

This activity shows clearly how certain linguistic choices made by the writer convey a strong impression of the Spanish as active, as causers of events, with Robbie as essentially a passive victim (see **2.2**).

Analysing linguistic choices   It will be observed that, in order to do Task 69, students need to see how particular linguistic choices made by a writer help to construct discourses which reflect beliefs and values, assumed to be shared with the model reader, in this case about the British and foreigners of which Robbie and the Spanish are representative. Rather than just focusing on form for its own sake however, as in traditional language and reading exercises, students can do so to adduce evidence for the way in which the writer prescribes for the reader a way of reading the text. One general aim of critical reading is to challenge such positionings by looking more closely at the means employed by the writer to construct discourses which work to the disadvantage of certain participants.

► **TASK 70**

Which linguistic choices made by the writers do you consider are significant in the treatment of the participants in this text and the accompanying rubric?

Part 5
Application of
reading strategies

The following passage is a complex descriptive passage. It is complex because it concerns a variety of aspects which are relevant to the description of a community. The passage describes a group of Indians living in a remote region of Colombia, South America. First make a list containing aspects that you would expect to find in the description of a primitive community. For example:

food
customs and beliefs

Then read the whole passage rapidly to find out which of the items in your list appear in the passage.
  Next read the passage carefully, paragraph by paragraph, in order to answer the comprehension questions. This will enable you to summarize the main aspects of the description. You do not need to complete all of the language study questions in the margins yet.

1
The picture shows a man rowing. What physical characteristic of the Noanamá results from rowing?

THE NOANAMÁ
The Noanamá are a handsome people; tallish and well-built with the heavy chest and shoulders of men accustomed to rowing;[1] their dark hair in a bowl-like fringe around the head; light-skinned, narrow-nosed and high-cheekboned, mongoloid in appearance with penetrating dark eyes. The women are often beautiful, with long flowing black hair and wearing no more than a cloth about their waist. Sometimes they put 'bija', a red dye, on their faces, and flowers in their hair. For ceremonies they cover their bodies with blue 'jagua' dye in a series of designs.[2]

(*Reading and Thinking in English* 1979:46–7)

One might wish to draw attention to the ways in which men and women are differentially described in this text (for example, 'people' in the first line co-refers with 'men' in the second). One might consider too the selection of physical attributes with which the text begins (rather than say, intellectual or religious characteristics). One kind of activity which might highlight the arguably racist and sexist discourse here, would be to consider the effect of replacing 'the Noanama' with a European group, such as 'the British' or 'the Germans'. Clearly specific lexis would change, so we might have something like: 'The British are a fair-skinned people; tallish and slightly built with the rounded shoulders of men accustomed to working long hours in the city ...'

Post-reading activities

Post-reading activities can serve the purpose of heightening the reader's awareness of other ways in which the topic could have been written about. One kind of activity which can offer this opportunity very readily is where two texts have been presented which deal with the same topic, but which draw on different discourses and imply a different model reader. For instance there are two versions of 'The Swallowing Drum', the story of Ndidi's journey into the forest quoted in Task 20. In one it is the heroine's mother who plans and brings about her daughter's rescue from the Swallowing Drum; in the other more typical version it is her father.

► TASK 71

Look at the follow-up activity to the reading of the two versions of the story 'The Swallowing Drum'. In what ways does this kind of task highlight for the reader significantly different features of two versions of a story?

The Two Stories	EXACTLY THE SAME	NEARLY THE SAME	DIFFERENT
In your pair or group, talk about the following questions on each story. Then decide if what happens in each story is EXACTLY THE SAME, NEARLY THE SAME or DIFFERENT, and put a tick in the right column.			
1. What is the name of the town where the story is set?			
2. What is the name of the main character?			
3. Who else is in the family?			
4. What jobs do the family members do?			
5. What does the main character want to do?			
6. Who tries to stop her doing what she wants to do? Why?			
7. How does the main character manage to leave home?			
8. Who does she meet on her way who is friendly?			
9. Who does she meet who is wicked?			
10. What does the evil drum do to people?			
11. What is the only way to escape from the evil drum?			
12. What happens to the main character when she meets the evil drum?			
13. What does the main character's Father do when he realises his daughter is a prisoner?			
14. What does the main character's Mother do when she realises her daughter is a prisoner?			
15. How does the main character escape?			
16. What happens to the wicked drum at the end of the story?			

(*Mellor and Raleigh, with Ashton 1984:21*)

This post-reading task draws attention to the different roles taken on by the participants in the two versions of the story, and is representative of the kind of task which might follow the reading of any text which contrasts in terms of genre, topic, or discourse.

11.4 Conclusion

To conclude, and by way of summing up some of the main issues presented in Section Two, I would like to suggest a classroom procedure which acknowledges the role of both context and content as socially determined, and which incorporates the role of textual information in supporting the interpretations we make.

First, students are given a whole text removed from its original context of use and asked to reconstruct what they can of the immediate, institutional, and wider social context.

▶   TASK 72

How far can you reconstruct the immediate, institutional, and wider social context of this text?

COLD WAR ENDS

Siberia will never be the same. Not with the Pelonis Ceramic Disc Furnace making peace between those who would have their rooms at different temperatures. Thermostatically controlled zone heating for the largest room in an average size home. 5200 BTUs of heat for about $1 per day. For the revolutionary dealer near you, call 1-800-872-7022.

P.S. A gift that will bring peace to your home.

THE ULTIMATE HEAT WAVE™
pelonis disc furnace

As a way of approaching this task, one could ask students to use the evidence available to them to suggest (1) the immediate context, i.e. where and when the text first appeared, who wrote it, and to whom it was addressed; (2) the institutional context, that is what social institutions are referred to, and (3) the broader social context which determines the particular kinds of discourses used to talk about the institutions. The reader needs to draw both from the text itself and various kinds of schematic knowledge to determine, for instance, that the text is addressed to a North American reader; that, institutionally, the text is recognizable as an advertisement and that the reader is therefore addressed as a consumer, but that other institutions are also referred to such as superpower politics ('cold war ends') and Christmas ('a gift that will bring peace to your home'). At the same time, the ways these are talked about indicate that certain views are taken for granted in the wider society. This brings us to consider the kinds of discourses embedded in the text.

Once broad answers to the questions about the context of the text have been established, one can look more closely at its content, that is the social meanings within the text and how these interact with the schematic knowledge which the reader brings to his or her reading of it. Here again the three questions suggested by Kress (see **2.2** and **11.3**) are useful as a way of looking more closely at the salient discourses. But an extra question should be added, to take account of readership, namely 'Who is the text's model reader (and therefore, by implication, who is excluded from this model readership)? Our stages then become:

1 Why is this topic being written about?
2 How is this topic being written about?
3 What other ways of writing about the topic are there?
4 Who is the text's model reader?

In answering these questions we need to draw partly on contextual knowledge, party on textual knowledge, and partly on schematic knowledge. At one level the answer to question 1 is straightforward, that is 'To sell a particular product', but at another level, related to question 2, we can consider why the producers of the text have chosen to relate the selling of a heating appliance to the discourse of world politics. This, in turn, relates to question 3, for there are clearly many different and certainly more direct ways to sell consumer goods. The choice of discourses selected in this particular text relates closely to a change in the range of discourses available to members of the wider North American society. At the time of writing there had been a radical change in the kind of discourses used in the West to describe East-West relations, explicitly signalled in this text by the phrase 'cold war ends'. In short, the text has been written in a context in which it is acceptable to talk positively about relations with the Soviet Union. Of course, if we turn to question 4, this discourse is only perceived as positive and optimistic to the text's model reader who is clearly from Western capitalist countries. The text is not, for instance, designed for a reader from the Soviet Union. Apart from obvious clues such as the choice of language and the price in dollars, the discourse revealed through 'Siberia will never be the same' is one designed for Western readers. Indeed, even though the next arguably forms part of the 'glasnost' genre which emerged during the early years of Gorbachev's leadership of the Soviet Union, and is—or is intended to be—read as pro-Soviet by Western readers, a reader from the former Soviet Union might find it offensive.

One might also draw students' attention to the presence of a conflict of discourses in the text, represented by a whole range of conflicting images and verbal expressions. For example the expression 'cold war' is in contrast to the smiling figure of the man and his conciliatory gesture. The reference to Siberia echoes 'cold' and is, for the Western reader, a place associated with conflict and dissidence. These ideas contrast with the notions of 'warmth' and 'peace' which the text also contains. And of course, crucial to the text's ultimate function, to sell a heating appliance, 'cold war ends' is also in contrast to 'the ultimate heatwave', an unconscious and ironic precursor of new discourses about the dangers of global warming and other environmental hazards which have largely replaced 'cold war' ones since this advertisement appeared in the United States in December 1987.

Exploring reading

12 Investigating reading in your own classroom

The tasks in **12** relate to some of the key principles introduced throughout this book and refer where appropriate to particular passages and tasks in Sections One and Two. Not all of them will be relevant to your setting, or kind and level of learner, so you are advised to use them selectively. The tasks progress from those which focus on the reader or learner reader (**12.1**), to those which focus on features of texts, including the role of context and discourse in the production and interpretation of texts (**12.2**), and those which focus on classroom reading procedures (**12.3**). The level of proficiency for which a task might be suitable is indicated.

12.1 Focus on the reader

▶ TASK 73

Aim
To establish the range of everyday experiences of reading in both the first and other languages of the group.

Level
All.

Resources
The discussion in **1.2**.

Procedure
1 Ask the class to note down everything they can remember reading the previous day, in any language. Ask them to include even minor reading events such as reading a shopping list or address book, and observing particular road signs.
2 Ask them to classify their reading under the following headings:
   – reading for survival (for example, road signs)
   – reading for learning (for example, an English grammar)
   – reading for pleasure (for example, a comic)
   – any other reasons
This activity could be done either individually or in groups.

Evaluation

1 What were the major differences and similarities between the experiences of different individuals or groups?

2 Can any implications be drawn for linking the kind of day-to-day reading done in the first language with that done in other languages, or in broadening the access to second language texts of different genres?

▶   TASK 74

Aim

To encourage students to reflect on and compare their roles, needs, and personal preferences as readers in their first language and in English.

Level

All.

Resources

Provide students with:

1 Model matrices which reflect either the first-language reading preferences of real or fictional people (see matrix A), or the day-to-day reading needs of a bi-literate learner (see matrix B).

2 A blank matrix based on A or B to complete.

WHO (readers)	WHAT (text types)	WHY (reasons for reading)	WHEN (time)	WHERE (place)
Jane	Science-fiction stories. Magazines and comics	Pleasure. Excitement. Escape to another world.	Any time she can find.	Travelling to work. At home.
Dave	Anything about the history of clocks.	Relaxation. Interest.	Evenings. Weekends.	At home. Library. Museum.
Alix	Non-fiction books about France and Germany – especially dictionaries.	Information. Help with her schoolwork.	Days, evenings. Not weekends.	At home At school.
Sam	Old maps and guides about the countryside.	Information. Pleasure. To find new places.	Any time.	At home. Places he visits.
Brenda and Max	Fashion magazines. Pop music papers.	Interest. Enjoyment. New ideas. To find jobs!	Brenda – all the time. Max – when not studying.	At home. At college. In class!
And what about you?				

Matrix A (*Davies and Whitney 1979:73*)

TABLE 1 *Literacy needs (Ravinder)*			
Literacy need	*Role of reader*	*Example of reading material*	*Likely language*
For:			
survival	e.g. motorist/pedestrian	Highway Code road signs	English
(basic day-to-day uses)	e.g. consumer	instructions on equipment	English
learning	student	textbooks, manuals	English
(especially skills)			
citizenship	e.g. supplementary benefit claimant	forms	English
(knowing about and acting on rights and duties)	e.g. well-informed member of the immediate community	local newspapers	Punjabi and English
	e.g. well-informed member of the wider community	national newspapers	English
maintaining	e.g. friend	letters	Punjabi
personal relationships	e.g. grandson		
personal pleasure	reader in purely personal capacity	comics, novels, magazines	Punjabi and some English

Matrix B (*Wallace 1988:8*)

Procedure

The students either complete a blank matrix themselves or interview each other in order to complete a profile of the reading activities of other class members. Lower-level learners could interview each other in their first language. Matrix B will be more appropriate where students are using two languages, at least one of them English, in day-to-day situations.

Evaluation

1 How many examples of different types of text were represented in the matrices?

2 Can any implications be drawn from the students reading preferences — that is their reading for pleasure — in planning texts and activities to promote reading for pleasure in the second language?

▶ ## TASK 75

Aim
To explore the reading histories of the group.

Level
Intermediate and advanced.

Resources

1 Texts which describe the reading histories of well-known people, such as the examples below. Alternatively, a more advanced class might produce their own reading histories. These, with the writers' permission, can then be used by other groups.

2 A matrix like the one below.

Only Connect

Labour MP for Brent South, Paul Boateng, talks to Chris Granlund about the way reading has influenced his life.

I learned to read in the Gold Coast, which later became Ghana. We used the self-same books that were being used in Britain, they simply transported the whole educational system and process. It's incredible but I didn't read an African book until I was 11 or 12. So my earliest recollections are of *Janet and John*. I also remember *Orlando the Marmalade Cat*, it was one of the first books that I borrowed from a library.

My grandfather was a great reader. He had left school at 14 and was a printer in East London. When I came back to see him during the holidays he would read *Treasure Island* to me. That's my earliest memory of a classic.

African Stars

Author Doris Lessing talks to Chris Granlund about the ways in which reading has influenced her life.

I remember sitting on the farm in Rhodesia and slowly piecing together the word c-i-g-a-r-e-t-t-e on the back of a cigarette packet and screaming, 'I can read! I can read!' And that was it. From then on I just read and read. My mother imported children's magazines from Britain, wonderful things like *Merry-Go-Round* that have just disappeared. The problem, of course, was that they were all about England and I was in Southern Rhodesia so I had this split going on right from the start. Every colonial or ex-colonial knows that it's hard to explain just what the split is.

In Plain English

Creator of Adrian Mole, playwright and novelist Sue Townsend, tells Chris Granlund about the growing pains of getting from the dunces' table to the top of the class.

I spent three miserable, lousy years at school with a teacher who used to slap my legs. And I couldn't learn to read. I just repeated *Janet and John* parrot fashion, sitting on the dunces' table. There was one teacher I adored. Mr Mole. He was a real eccentric. Taking the register in the morning he would suddenly break into an Irish folk song. In the afternoons, before we went home, he would read to us. He read a lot of Dickens, *Winnie the Pooh*, *Tom Sawyer*, all kinds of books.

The school was in the middle of a posh area. Most of the children lived in huge houses with huge gardens but we lived in a little prefab. The prefabs were all in a circle and they were called the rabbit hutches. Both my parents were on the buses at the time. They always went off to work with a book in their changebags. They were very literate and both of them used to read at least four library books every week.

(*Marxism Today*, June, August, October 1989)

FIRST MEMORIES OF READING (what, where, with whom?)			
FAVOURITE READING AS A CHILD (books, authors, genres)			
FAVOURITE READING AS AN ADULT (books, authors, genres)			
MOST IMPORTANT BOOK/S OR AUTHOR/S IN YOUR LIFE			
MAIN ROLES AND PURPOSES OF READING (e.g. as parent, for pleasure)			

Procedure

1 The class read one, or several, of the reading histories with a view to completing the matrix.

2 Where possible, they ask another English-speaking person the same questions.

3 Students then either record their own reading histories or that of a partner in the class.

4 Individuals report back on their findings and the class discuss what the reading profiles reveal about educational background, gender, and nationality as well as personality.

Evaluation

How far were the students able to draw implications from the reading histories about the social roles associated with the reading experiences and behaviour of the people described?

▶ ## TASK 76

Aim

To highlight the existence of different literacies related to different reading experiences which students bring with them from their own cultural context, as well as those developed in a second language context.

Level

Advanced.

Resources

The discussion in 3.3.

Procedure

1 Conduct a guided discussion in which students are asked to try and identify different kinds of literacies related to English and to their first language, for example computer literacy, consumer literacy, religious literacy, academic literacy.

2 Ask them to consider which literacies in which language play a role in their own lives, and what kinds of reading strategies they involve. For example, 'consumer literacy' involves scanning for products in mail order catalogues or supermarkets; 'academic literacy' involves making use of indices and contents pages.

Evaluation

Did any observations emerge which would help to account for difficulties in dealing with literacy events in English as opposed to the students' first languages?

▶ TASK 77

Aim

To encourage students to reflect on their second-language reading strategies and to consider ways of improving them.

Level

Intermediate and advanced.

Resources

1 Various texts representing different genres, for example, 'menu', 'short story', 'news article', 'personal letter', brought into class either by the teacher or the students themselves.

2 A simple chart based on the examples from Ellis and Sinclair (1989) given below.

Procedure

1 Students select a text for reading in the classroom and decide what strategies will be involved in reading it, for example, reading for detail or scanning to find specific information.

2 They read the text and complete the chart, making their own assessment of success based on the particular strategies they were assessing (as indicated in the middle column of the chart).

3 They might be encouraged to continue this process of self-assessment by completing a similar chart when reading various texts at home in their own time.

Evaluation

How aware are students of the range of possible reader strategies and their own strengths and weaknesses as readers?

Name: *Erik*

Date	Activity/Situation	Points to assess	Assessment
6.1.88	*Reading newspaper article on sport*	*Speed* *Understanding of main ideas (skimming)*	*2 mins. 50 secs.* *60% of main ideas!* *Speed! Still trying to read every word!*

Name: *Sofia*

Date	Activity/Situation	Points to assess	Assessment
9.4.88	*Reading User Guide for my home computer*	*Reading for detail*	*Not very good.* *Must learn some more computer vocabulary before I try again.* *Must find out more about how computers work in general.*

(*Ellis and Sinclair 1989:85*)

▶ TASK 78

Aim
To encourage students to read for pleasure.

Level
All, apart from absolute beginners.

Resources
Books brought in by students or made available from a class library.

Procedure
1 Each student in turn reports on a book that he or she is currently reading in English. This may be a book in its original version, a simplified version published as a graded reader, or an original story in a series of graded readers (see the discussion in 9). Students comment on genre, topic, readership, and for what occasion they would recommend the book; for example, a stay in hospital, a long plane journey, a summer holiday.

2 They might then produce cards to be filed and consulted by other members of the class like the one below.

Title	Genre	Topic	Readership	Occasion
Bloodlust	ghost story	vampires	teenagers	not when alone!

Evaluation
The teacher can take notes of individual students' reading preferences, and whether they are ambitiously reading beyond their general reading proficiency, or the reverse. What implications are there for activities within the classroom designed to encourage the enjoyment of literature written in the second language?

12.2 Focus on the text

▶ TASK 79

Aim
To establish the importance of situational and textual context in interpreting texts.

Level
Intermediate to advanced.

Resources
Different short texts which are presented to the students divorced from textual and situational contexts (see, for example, the texts in Task 14 and the messages in Task 16).

Procedure

1 Ask students to reconstruct the context by deciding on the writer, the model reader, the setting, and the purpose. With some texts one can also invite conjecture regarding the institutional and wider social context as discussed in **4**. So, to take a simple example, for the short text, DINOSAUR TRACKS, we might have:
   - Immediate context—written by someone in an official capacity for the public at large to provide information in a public place, possibly a museum.
   - Institutional context—educational; the phenomenon is considered to be of historical interest; people may pay an entrance fee to see the exhibit referred to.
   - Wider social context—a society where historical evidence is valued and artefacts are collected and made available to the public.

2 Give students the original context in which the text occurred and invite them to compare it with their own predictions.

Evaluation

What kinds of evidence do students draw on? In some cases they will be strongly dependent on background knowledge of the world, as in the example given; in others, they will be more dependent on the evidence of the language in the text itself.

▶ # TASK 80

Aim

To encourage students to appreciate features of cohesion in texts, especially the way in which form relates to propositional meaning and communicative function.

Level

Advanced.

Resources

Texts which present problems of cohesion in various ways (see, for example, the discussion in **2.1** and Task 7).

Procedure

Students discuss in what ways the texts are odd or unexpected in the manner in which sections of the texts relate to each other formally, semantically, or functionally. In doing so they can be encouraged to develop metalinguistic knowledge (see **7.4**) by using terms such as 'pronoun', 'article', and 'connector'.

Evaluation

Did the activity encourage metalinguistic awareness through contextualizing the use of linguistic terms which describe the operation of cohesion? As argued in the discussion of Task 69, an understanding of the effect of cohesive features can also be applied to critical analyses of the discourses within texts.

► TASK 81

Aim
To sensitize students to the concept of discourse, as introduced in **2.2**.

Level
Advanced.

Resources
Sets of simple children's books in English (and other languages, where possible).

Procedure
In the context of a general discussion about children's books (of interest to adult learners, especially if they are parents or teachers) introduce students to ways in which salient discourses in texts relate to social institutions such as the family, schooling, and social class. The discourses which reflect these institutions tend to be clearly signalled in children's books, especially the allocation of family roles.

Evaluation
Were the students able to notice any clear differences between the different books in the ways social institutions are talked about, for example, in the case of families, the family roles of mothers and fathers, and boys and girls?

► TASK 82

Aim
To make students aware of the ways in which both textual and discourse features typify certain genres.

Level
Intermediate to advanced.

Resources
1 The discussion in 5.
2 The openings of different texts, for example, a novel, a newspaper article, a personal letter, and a business letter.

Procedure
1 Get students to attempt to identify the genres which the texts belong to. They can first be asked to comment on the nature of the textual evidence they can draw on, for example, syntactic features such as the presence of subordinate clauses, or particular uses of the article or passive voice.

2 Ask students to look at discourse features, for example, ways of talking about women in, say, a romantic novel as compared to a newspaper article from the quality press, with a view to commenting on how typical they are of the genre.

Evaluation
How successful were the students in identifying the genres? Which were the most reliable clues on which they drew?

12.3 Focus on classroom reading procedures

▶ TASK 83

Aim
To encourage students to be aware of the intended readership of texts, and of their producers in terms of writers, publishers, and proprietors.

Level
Intermediate and advanced.

Resources
A range of texts, for example, newspapers, magazines, leaflets, advertisements, appeals for charities, political literature, and EFL material of all kinds. Where possible students should be encouraged to bring in this material themselves.

Procedure
1 Divide the class into groups and give each group a mixed set of texts.
2 Each group sorts its texts into different categories. Examples of categories might be: professional reading material; public information leaflets; advertisements.
3 When the students have identified five or six broad types of text they attempt to establish the following for each type:
   – Who produces them?
   – For whom are they produced?
   – Why have they been produced?
   – Is this type of text of interest/relevance to you? Why/why not?

Evaluation
Did the activity make the students more aware, not just of model readers for different types of text, but of the range of producers of texts?

► ## TASK 84

Aim
To encourage students to predict outcomes in narratives by drawing on schematic knowledge of the genre.

Level
All.

Resources
Any narrative text, preferably a folk tale like 'The Swallowing Drum' (see Task 20).

Procedure
1 Ask students to pick out a key phrase or sentence from the early part of the text which anticipates the outcome of the story. An example in the case of 'The Swallowing Drum' might be 'she was particularly precious to them'.

2 Discuss or compare different options.

3 The students read the story to see if their expectations are confirmed.

Evaluation
1 Was it possible to reach a consensus on what might constitute a key phrase or sentence?

2 Was this activity successful in encouraging students to draw on their schematic knowledge for story genres and to anticipate the outcome of the story?

► ## TASK 85

Aim
To encourage students to draw on schematic knowledge about the role of characters in stories.

Level
All.

Resources
Any story genre, for example, folk tale, soap opera, romantic novel, thriller.

Procedure
1 Give the students a list of characters in a story.

2 Ask them to work in groups to guess the development of the story. Make sure they involve all the characters.

3 Get them to compare their own versions of the story with the actual one.

Evaluation
How similar were the stories produced by the groups? If you are teaching in a multicultural group, could any differences be attributable to culturally variable discourses within the same genre?

▶ TASK 86

Aim
To show students how the information in texts with different topics but shared propositional content and communication function may be characterized in similar ways.

Level
Intermediate to advanced.

Resources
1 The discussion in **10.2**.
2 A set of texts which share the same communicative function, for example, 'describing people' or 'reporting a series of events'.

Procedure
Design matrices or diagrams which can capture the characteristics of different text-types. An example for 'reporting a series of events' might be a time-line, on which key events are recorded in the order in which they occurred.

Evaluation
1 How far is it possible to characterize other text-types by matrices?
2 Could your students be encouraged to design their own?

▶ TASK 87

Aim
To encourage students to build up information about a text's authorship, readership, topic, genre, and purpose by identifying salient discourses within it.

Level
Advanced.

Resources
1 A text which divides naturally into three or four separate sections.
2 A matrix as shown below (this was completed by a student in an advanced class while reading a newspaper article by Mrs Thatcher).

Procedure
1 Present students with successive chunks of text, but withhold all information regarding source, topic, headline, and author until the end of the activity.
2 Give each student a matrix similar to that below to make any notes after reading each section of the text, or to amend an impression given by a previous extract. A tick indicates that the student does not wish to make any amendment to his or her existing judgement.

Deducing information from text extracts and predicting

	Section 1	Section 2	Section 3
1 What is the genre?	*Magazine article (own experience)*	✓	*An issue of Onward a Conservative Party publication (women in general)*
2 Why was it written?	*To inform people of the change of women*	*To help women understand that is possible to be both a career woman and housewife*	✓
3 What is the topic?	*Women nowadays*	✓	*Mother knows best*
4 Who is writing? (i.e. gender, class, nationality) + personal traits?	*A woman middle class English demanding person*	✓	*Margaret Thatcher*
5 To or for whom is he/she writing?	*Every adult whole society*	*Specifically to women*	*Whole society*
6 What other information is revealed by the text e.g. time of writing	*80's*	*Late 80's*	*1954!!!*

After each section pause to ask a question / questions of the author which you feel the text raises, e.g.
- *Can she be a mother and a career woman?*
- *What is the role of the man?*

Evaluation
1 How well were the students able to draw on clues provided by discourses within the text in order to construct an author and a model reader, as well as the text's topic, genre, and purpose?

2 What are the implications for creating tasks which focus on this area?

▶   TASK 88

Aim
To show how texts relate to a context of use, as well as a context of production, and how different texts will be consulted in different phases of an event.

Level
Intermediate to advanced.

Resources
Sets of texts which relate to an event, for example, going to the theatre, making a school trip, buying a new car, going on holiday.

Procedure
Replicate in the classroom the contexts of use of texts which relate to an event. This can be done within a pre-/while-/post-reading procedure. For example, discussion of criteria for choosing a car might form one pre-reading activity, along with the scanning of newspaper advertisements. Reading a car manual might involve a while-reading exercise of matching a set of instructions to a diagram. A post-reading activity might be writing a letter of complaint about the car itself or the instructions in the manual.

Evaluation
It is possible to plan a whole reading course around events and the reading needs they involve? What might the difficulties be?

▶   TASK 89

Aim
To encourage the integration of language modes through role-play, as part of post-reading.

Level
Intermediate and advanced.

Resources
1 A text which presents a number of participants as witnesses to, or as involved in, a controversial event or situation. 'The blame that Spain must share' (page 16) is a possible example.
2 The role play described in the follow-up to Task 58.

Procedure
1 Give students role-play cards which represent alternative roles for the character. For example, 'You are Robbie's girlfriend. You agree that he is basically decent and you want to defend his behaviour.' Another possible role is two versions of Robbie himself, for example a contrite and a defiant one.
2 Students prepare notes in their respective roles and then present their viewpoint to the rest of the class.

Evaluation

1 Do students respond well to role-play activities based on texts of this kind?

2 What other genres lend themselves to role-play?

► TASK 90

Aim

To encourage students to raise questions rather than answer them as part of pre-reading, i.e. to encourage a problem-posing rather than a problem-solving approach.

Level

Advanced.

Resources

Controversial topical texts, or texts which encode an experience relevant to a particular group of learners, for example, an issue of global relevance such as the environment. These should be brought in to class by the students themselves if possible.

Procedure

Ask students to skim the text with a view to stating the problem or set of problems it represents for them: for example, 'The excessive consumption of resources by the developed countries'. Alternatively an initial skim may raise questions, for example: 'Why are the effects of pollution worse in some places than in others?' Students then read the text more closely with the aim of answering their questions and raising further questions with which they can approach other texts dealing with the same or similar issues.

Evaluation

1 What kind of texts do students choose to bring into the classroom?

2 Is it possible to find texts which act as codes for a whole class or are their experiences and attitudes too diverse?

► TASK 91

Aim

To use a literary text as a code; to encourage students to produce creative texts such as simple poems which may provide the basis of a set of texts for other learners.

Level

Intermediate and advanced.

Resources
A single poem or a collection by one or several writers. Examples might be the poems by Grace Nichols in Task 38 and by Priscilla Dube in Task 61.

Procedure
1 Read a poem which is likely to have a resonance for your students, that is to offer a potential set of interpretations which will be close to their personal and social experiences.

2 Ask the students to write their own texts. These may take the same theme but change the genre, or keep the genre but change the theme. Thus, if you read Priscilla Dube's poem to them, students could write a short narrative about naming rather than a poem, or, on analogy with the Black Poem quoted in Task 38, a Fat Poem could be composed with the same verse form and rhyme.

Evaluation
How willing are students to create their own texts, especially if they deal with personal feelings? Some students find poems a very natural medium; others will prefer prose. In some teaching contexts student-produced texts make highly motivating reading material for other learners.

▶ TASK 92

Aim
To encourage students to reflect on the options writers have in how they choose to write about a topic.

Level
Intermediate and advanced.

Resources
The discussion in **11.3**. Any non-fiction text.

Procedure
1 As part of pre-reading, ask the students to establish, through an initial skim read, what they think the topic of the text is (they may agree or disagree with the actual title or any headings given).

2 Ask them to brainstorm the range of ways in which this topic might be tackled.

3 As a post-reading activity, students can consider which options were, and which were not, taken up by the writer.

Evaluation
1 How far were the students able to think of other kinds of discourses than those selected by the writer?

2 What implications were they able to draw about the discourse choices actually made?

► TASK 93

Aim
To encourage students to see how parallel discourses may develop through the same text, and how they are frequently in opposition to each other.

Level
Advanced.

Resources
1 The discussion in **2.2.**

2 Any text which includes two sets of protagonists, for example, two football teams, two individuals, two political groups, opponents in a conflict or war.

Procedure
1 Ask students to trace through the text the sets of collocations linked to each protagonist.

2 The lists produced are then compared and discussed. Students can be asked to think of synonyms or near-synonyms to replace the writer's actual lexical choices and to compare the effect of these replacements with the original items.

Evaluation
Did the task highlight for the learners ways in which participants in texts may be given 'unequal treatment'?

► TASK 94

Aim
To encourage students to explore critically the discourse in minimal texts such as advertisements or leaflets.

Level
Intermediate and advanced.

Resources
1 The discussion in **11.4.**

2 An advertisement such as that reproduced in Task 10.

Procedure
1 Take the four key questions given in **11.4**:
   - Why is this topic being written about?
   - How is this topic being written about?
   - What other ways of writing about the topic are there?
   - Who is the text's model reader?

2 Ask the students to use these questions as a basis for:
   − exploring the overall function of the text
   − discussing which discourses the text has drawn upon
   − considering discourses which might have been drawn upon
   − deciding who the text is primarily addressed to.

Evaluation

What insights does this procedure offer second language learners into ways that writers—of persuasive texts in particular—position readers through the selection of one set of discourses rather than another?

Glossary

authentic texts: real-life texts, not written for pedagogic purposes.

bottom-up processing: ways of reading texts which attend to linguistic forms at the level of words or sentences.

closed texts: texts which encourage a conformist and restricted interpretation of textual meaning.

cloze procedure: a procedure which involves the deletion of words in a text at regular intervals, used either for checking the readability of texts or, as part of both teaching and testing procedures, for encouraging learners to draw on the surrounding context to guess the meaning of the missing items.

coherence: the manner in which parts of texts can be meaningfully related to other parts, even in the absence of linguistic connectors.

cohesion: the formal links between sentences and within sentences.

collocation: strong conventional association between two or more language items, for example 'fish and chips', 'man and wife'.

communicative function: the use of certain forms of language in parts of texts or whole texts which, when account is taken of the context, allows the reader to recognize a particular intent on the part of the writer, for example, to persuade, to congratulate, to instruct.

discourses: ways of talking or writing about phenomena, events, or social relationships which reflect conventional ways of doing things in a particular society, as determined by its major social institutions.

environmental print: printed messages which we see around us in everyday settings.

genre: a text-type which has a distinctive form and content and which is socioculturally recognizable as serving a particular function, for example, 'short story', 'business letter', 'theatre programme'.

graphophonic cues: information in texts based on relationships between spelling and sound which allows the reader to understand the text.

interpretative community: a social group which shares ways of interpreting texts.

intertextuality: the way in which our production and interpretation of texts is dependent on our knowledge of other texts.

language experience approaches: approaches where a student's own language and experiences form the basis of a written text, either written by him or herself, or by the teacher acting as scribe.

literacy events: day-to-day events which involve reading and writing, often in interaction with other people.

look and say method: a method in initial reading which focuses on word recognition by, for example, asking learners to name words presented on flash cards.

metacognition: the awareness of one's own learning and thinking processes.

metalanguage: the use of linguistic terms to describe language data, for example terms such as 'pronoun', 'article', and 'perfect aspect'.

miscues: cases where, in reading aloud, the observed response is different from the expected response, that is the actual word or words on the page.

model reader: the kind of reader, defined, for instance, in terms of gender, class, and nationality, which a writer has in mind when constructing a text.

open texts: texts which allow the reader a wide range of choices in how they might be interpreted.

phonic method: a method in initial reading which involves asking the learner to match up letters to a sound representation.

positioning: the way in which a writer invites a reader to adopt a particular point of view about the issues dealt with in the text.

problem-posing: an approach to reading in which texts are used which encode experiences with which a particular group of learners can identify and which present problems, usually of a social nature.

process approach: an approach to reading which is concerned with the manner in which meaning is created by the reader in the course of reading.

product approach: an approach to reading which is concerned with what the reader has 'got out of the text'; the text is seen as an object from which meaning can be extracted.

propositional meaning: the way in which ideas or concepts are conveyed in a text.

schema: a mental model which we use to relate new to already known information. We do this in ways which are socioculturally influenced.

semantic cues: textual information which allows the reader to predict the continuation of the text by drawing on his or her knowledge of the meaning of words and the *collocational* constraints regarding the kinds of words that typically occur with others.

skills/subskills: supposed sets of specific abilities which are built up sequentially, higher ones depending on lower ones, to produce a particular kind of behaviour; a skills approach to teaching involves the division of language data into manageable chunks.

strategies: ways of reading which are employed flexibly and selectively and which vary depending on the text-type, and the context and purpose of reading; a strategy approach to teaching reading is concerned with the ways in which the reader processes the text.

syntactic cues: information in the text which allows the reader to predict the continuation of the text on the basis of his or her knowledge of English syntax, for example of typical word order.

text: a unified piece of language which carries a whole meaning and has a communicative function.

top-down processing: ways of reading texts which attend to global meaning and are activated largely by existing knowledge of the world rather than the specific linguistic features of the text.

Further Reading

Alderson, C. and **A. Urquhart.** (eds.) 1984. *Reading in a Foreign Language.* London: Longman.
An excellent collection of research papers which cover a wide area of interest, though the emphasis is on reading for formal learning. The full introduction and the postscripts to each contribution make useful links across the different papers.

Anderson, A. and **T. Lynch.** 1988. *Listening.* Oxford: Oxford University Press.
Many of the principles laid down in this book apply equally well to reading. This book complements and extends areas dealt with in *Reading.*

Auerbach, E. and **N. Wallerstein.** 1987. *English for the Workplace. ESL for Action: Problem Posing at Work.* Wokingham: Addison Wesley.
This is an excellent coursebook designed for ESL learners in work situations. It is full of innovative ideas for the development of language and literacy, and uses a problem-posing approach. The Teachers' Book gives a particularly clear rationale of ways in which Freirean principles can be applied to ESL practice.

Cook, G. 1989. *Discourse.* Oxford: Oxford University Press.
Cook provides a lucid account of both formal features of texts and different models of discourse. Many of the tasks in the book relate to the reading process and thus are complementary to the kinds of tasks presented in *Reading.*

Ellis, G. and **B. Sinclair** 1989. *Learning to Learn English.* Cambridge: Cambridge University Press.
This learner-training material offers practical ways in which learners can evaluate and record their own learning strategies, including their reading strategies. It illustrates very effectively how a concern with learning processes, as well as products, can be implemented in the classroom.

Kress, G. 1989. *Linguistic Processes in Sociocultural Practice.* Oxford: Oxford University Press.
This book offers a framework for critical reading along with some ways of applying it to different kinds of texts, in particular educational texts for school-age children and media texts.

Wallace, C. 1988. *Learning to Read in a Multicultural Society: The Social Context of Second Language Literacy.* New York: Prentice Hall. This book takes a case-study approach to the discussion of initial reading for adults and children who are acquiring English language literacy in an English speaking environment.

Bibliography

Alderson, C. and A. Urquhart (eds.) 1984. *Reading in a Foreign Language.* London: Longman.

Andersen, R. 1988a. 'Overwriting and other techniques for success with academic articles' in *Academic Writing: Process and Product.* London: Modern English Publications in association with the British Council.

Andersen, R. 1988b. *The Power and the Word.* London: Paladin.

Anderson, A. and T. Lynch. 1988. *Listening* in 'Language Teaching: A Scheme for Teacher Education'. Oxford: Oxford University Press.

Aston, G. 1979. 'Communicative competence and reading.' *Lingua e nuova didattica* 3: 22–4.

Auerbach, E. and N. Wallerstein. 1987. *English for the Workplace. ESL for Action: Problem Posing at Work.* Wokingham: Addison Wesley.

Barr, P., J. Clegg, and C. Wallace. 1981. *Advanced Reading Skills.* London: Longman.

Breen, M. 1985. 'Authenticity in the language classroom' in *Applied Linguistics* 6/1: 60–9.

Brice-Heath, S. 1983. *Ways with Words.* Cambridge: Cambridge University Press.

Brieger, N. and A. Jackson. 1989. *Advanced International English.* London: Cassell.

Brown, G. and G. Yule. 1983. *Discourse Analysis.* Cambridge: Cambridge University Press.

Brusch, W. 1991. 'The role of reading in foreign language acquisition: designing an experimental project.' *ELT Journal* 45/2.

Buck, C. 1979. 'Miscues of non-native speakers of English' in K. Goodman (ed.): *Miscue Analysis.* Urbana, Ill.: ERIC Clearinghouse on Reading and Communication Skills.

Carrell, P. 1988. 'Interactive text processing: implications for ESL/second language reading classrooms' in P. Carrell, J. Devine, and D. Eskey (eds.): *Interactive Approaches to Second Language Reading.* Cambridge: Cambridge University Press.

Carrell, P. 1991. 'Second language reading: reading ability or language proficiency?' *Applied Linguistics* 12/2: 159–79.

Carrell, P., J. Devine, and D. Eskey (eds.) 1988. *Interactive Approaches to Second Language Reading.* Cambridge: Cambridge University Press.

Cavalcanti, M. 1987. 'Investigating FL reading performance through pause protocols' in C. Færch and G. Kasper (eds.): *Introspection in Second Language Research.* Bristol: Multilingual Matters.

Clark, M. 1976. *Young Fluent Readers*. London: Heinemann Educational.

Cook, G. 1989. *Discourse* in 'Language Teaching: A Scheme for Teacher Education'. Oxford: Oxford University Press.

Cummins, J. 1979. 'Linguistic interdependence and the educational development of bilingual children.' *Review of Educational Research* 49/2: 222–51.

Cummins, J. and **M. Swain.** 1986. *Bilingualism in Education*. London: Longman.

Davies, E. and **N. Whitney.** 1979. *Reasons for Reading*. London: Heinemann Educational.

Davies, F. 1982. Workshop at a conference entitled 'The Effective Use of Reading'. National Association for Remedial Education, Chester College of Higher Education.

de Beaugrande, R. and **W. Dressler.** 1981. *Introduction to Text Linguistics*. London: Longman.

Doughty, C. and **T. Pica.** 1986. 'Information gap tasks: do they facilitate second language acquisition?' *TESOL Quarterly*. 20/2: 305–24.

Dubin, F. 1989. 'The odd couple: reading and vocabulary'. *ELT Journal* 43/4.

Eagleton, T. 1983. *Literary Theory*. Oxford: Blackwell.

Eco, U. 1981. *The Role of the Reader: Explorations in the Semiotics of Texts*. London: Hutchinson.

Eckstut, S. and **D. Lubelska.** 1989. *Beneath the Surface*. London: Longman.

Elley, W. B. 1984. 'Exploring the reading difficulties of second-language readers in Fiji' in C. Alderson and A. Urquhart (eds.).

Ellis, G. and **B. Sinclair.** 1989. *Learning to Learn English: A Course in Learner Training*. Cambridge: Cambridge University Press.

Eskey, D. 1988. 'Holding in the bottom' in Carrell, P., J. Devine, and D. Eskey (eds.): *Interactive Approaches to Second Language Reading*. Cambridge: Cambridge University Press.

Fairclough, N. 1989. *Language and Power*. London: Longman.

Fish, S. 1980. *Is There a Text in This Class? The Authority of Interpretative Communities*. Boston, Mass.: Harvard University Press.

Foll, D. 1990. *Contrasts: Developing Text Awareness*. London: Longman.

Freire, P. 1976. *Education: The Practice of Freedom*. London: Writers and Readers Publishing Cooperative.

Fry, E. 1977. 'Fry's readability graph: clarification, validity, and extension to level 17.' *Journal of Reading* 20: 242–52.

Gill, V. 1969. *Read, Think and Choose*. London: Duckworth.

Gilroy, B. 1975. *Rice and Peas*. Basingstoke: Macmillan Education.

Goodman, K. 1967. 'Reading: a psycholinguistic guessing game' in F. K. Gollasch (ed.): *Language and Literacy: The Collected Writings of Kenneth S. Goodman*. Vol 1: Process, Theory, Research. London: Routledge, 1982.

Goodman, K. 1984. 'Unity in reading' in *Becoming Readers in a Complex Society: Eighty-third Year Book of the National Society for the Study of Education*. Chicago: National Society for the Study of Education.

Goodman, K. 1987. Lecture on 'Reading as a psycholinguistic process' at the University of Arizona.

Goodman, K., L. Bridges Bird, and **Y. Goodman.** 1991. *The Whole Language Catalog.* Santa Rosa, Ca.: American School Publishers.

Gumperz, J. J. 1972. 'Introduction' in J. J. Gumperz and D. Hymes (eds.): *Directions in Sociolinguistics.* New York: Holt, Rinehart, and Winston.

Guozhang, X. 1986. *CECL (Communicative English for Chinese Learners): Core Course 2.* Peking: China National Publishing Corporation.

Halliday, M. A. K. 1978. *Language as Social Semiotic.* London: Edward Arnold.

Halliday, M. A. K. and **R. Hasan.** 1985. *Language, Context and Text: Aspects of Language in a Social-semiotic Perspective.* Oxford: Oxford University Press.

Hedge, T. 1988. *Guidelines to Oxford Bookworms.* Oxford: Oxford University Press.

Horsburgh, D. 1982. *Druk Readers Book Four.* Delhi: Oxford University Press.

Hosenfeld, C. 1977. 'A preliminary investigation of the reading strategies of successful and non-successful second language learners.' *System 5*: 110–23.

Hosenfeld, C. 1984. 'Case studies of ninth grade readers' in Alderson and Urquhart 1984.

Hutchinson, T. and **A. Waters.** 1985. *English for Specific Purposes: A Learning-centred Approach.* Cambridge: Cambridge University Press.

Johns, T. and **F. Davies.** 1983. 'Text as a vehicle for information: the classroom use of written texts in teaching reading in a foreign language.' *Reading in a Foreign Language* 1/1: 1–20.

Kress, G. 1985. *Linguistic Processes in Sociocultural Practice.* Oxford: Oxford University Press.

Laird, E. 1978. *The House on the Hill.* Heinemann Guided Readers Series. London: Heinemann Educational.

Lindop, C. and **D. Fisher.** 1988. *Something to Read.* Cambridge: Cambridge University Press.

Lunzer, E. and **K. Gardner.** 1979. *The Effective Use of Reading.* London: Heinemann Educational Books for the Schools Council.

Mackay, D., B. Thompson, and **P. Schaub.** 1970. *Breakthrough to Literacy Teachers Manual: The Theory and Practice of Teaching Initial Reading and Writing.* London: Longman for the Schools Council.

Martin, J. R., F. Christie, and **J. Rothery.** 1987. 'Social processes in education: a reply to Sawyer and Watson (and others)' in I. Reid (ed.): *The Place of Genre in Learning: Current Debates.* Victoria, Australia: Deakin University Centre of Studies in Literary Education.

McRae, J. and **L. Pantaleoni.** 1990. *Chapter and Verse: An Interactive Approach to Literature.* Oxford: Oxford University Press.

Meinhof, U. 1987. 'Predicting aspects of a strategic model of text comprehension' in T. Bloor and J. Norrish (eds.): *Written Language.* London: CILT.

Mellor, B., J. Hemming, and J. Leggett. 1984. *Changing Stories*. London: The English Centre.

Mellor, B., M. O'Neill, and A. Patterson. 1987. *Reading Stories*. London: The English Centre.

Mellor, B., M. Raleigh, and P. Ashton. 1984. *Making Stories*. London: The English Centre.

Molteno Project. 1987. *Bridge Plus One: Pupil's Book*. Institute for the Study of English in Africa. Pretoria: De Jager-Haum.

Nichols, G. 1984. *The Fat Black Woman's Poems*. London: Virago.

Nystrand, M. 1986. *The Structure of Written Communication: Studies in Reciprocity between Writers and Readers*. Orlando, Fla.: Academic Press.

Olson, D. 1977. 'From utterance to text: the bias of language in speech and writing.' *Harvard Educational Review* 47/3: 257–81.

Reading and Thinking in English. 1980. *Book 1: Concepts in Use*. Oxford: Oxford University Press.

Reading and Thinking in English. 1979. *Book 2: Exploring Functions*. Oxford: Oxford University Press.

Reading and Thinking in English. 1979. *Book 3: Discovering Discourse*. Oxford: Oxford University Press.

Rigg, P. 1986. 'Reading in ESL: learning from kids' in *Children and ESL: Integrating Perspectives*. Washington, DC: TESOL.

Rossner, R. 1988. *The Whole Story*. London: Longman.

Savage, K. L., M. How, and E. Yeung. 1982. *English that Works*. Palo Alto, Ca.: Scott Foresman.

Scholes, R. 1985. *Textual Power*. New Haven, Conn.: Yale University Press.

Simatupang, M. and A. Aryanto. 1988. *Bahasa Inggris 1a*. Jakarta: Sekolah Menengah Atas Departemen Pendidikan dan Kebudayaan.

Smith, F. 1971. *Understanding Reading: a Psycholinguistic Analysis of Reading and Learning to Read*. Orlando, Fla.: Holt, Reinhart, and Winston.

Smith, F. 1983. *The Promise and Threat of Microcomputers for Language Learners*. Washington, DC: TESOL.

Stannard-Allen, W., M. El-Anani, and Y. Salah. 1970. *New Living English for Jordan* Books 1 and 5. Ministry of Education, Jordan.

Steffenson, M. S., C. Joag-Dev, and R. C. Anderson. 1979. 'A cross-cultural perspective on reading comprehension.' *Reading Research Quarterly* 15/1: 10–29.

Stinton, J. (ed). 1979. *Racism and Sexism in Children's Books*. London: Writers and Readers Publishing Cooperative.

Stubbs, M. 1980. *Language and Literacy: The Sociolinguistics of Reading and Writing*. London: Routledge and Kegan Paul.

Street, B. 1984. *Literacy in Theory and Practice*. Cambridge: Cambridge University Press.

Swales, J. 1990. *Genre Analysis: English in Academic and Research Settings*. Cambridge: Cambridge University Press.

Tomlinson, B. and R. Ellis. 1988. *Reading: Advanced*. Oxford: Oxford University Press.

Wallace, C. 1987. 'The representation of spoken language in early reading books: problems for early L2 readers' in T. Bloor and J. Norrish (eds.): *Written Language*. London: CILT.

Wallace, C. 1988. *Learning to Read in a Multicultural Society: The Social Context of Second Language Literacy*. New York: Prentice Hall.

Wallace, C. and Y. Goodman. 1989. 'Research currents: language and literacy development of multilingual learners.' *Language Arts* 66/5: 524–41.

Walter, C. 1982. *Authentic Reading*. Cambridge: Cambridge University Press.

Weaver, C. 1980. *Psycholinguistics and Reading: From Process to Practice*. Cambridge, Mass.: Winthrop Publishers.

Widdowson, H. G. 1975. *Stylistics and the Teaching of Literature*. London: Longman.

Widdowson, H. G. 1978. *Teaching Language as Communication*. Oxford: Oxford University Press.

Widdowson, H. G. 1979. 'Discourse and text.' Paper given at Ealing College of Higher Education Conference on 'The Reading Skill'.

Widdowson, H. G. 1983. *Learning Purpose and Language Use*. Oxford: Oxford University Press.

Widdowson, H. G. 1984. 'Reading and Communication' in C. Alderson and A. Urquhart 1984.

Williams, E. 1984. *Reading in the Language Classroom*. London: Macmillan.

Zimbabwe School Readers Series. 1986. *Young Voices*.

Index

Entries relate to Sections One, Two, and Three of the text, and to the glossary. References to the glossary are indicated by 'g' after the page number.

Acknowledgements

The publishers and authors would like to thank the following for their kind permission to use articles, extracts, or illustrations from copyright material. There are instances where we have been unable to trace or contact the copyright holder before our printing deadline. We apologize for this apparent negligence. If notified the publisher will be pleased to rectify any errors of omissions at the earliest opportunity.

Addison Wesley for an extract from *English for the Workplace. ESL for Action: Problem Posing at Work* (1987) by E. Auerbach and N. Wallerstein.

The British Council for extracts from *Reading and Thinking in English* (1979 and 1980).

British Telecom for permission to reproduce the advertisement 'A simple call could save your liver and bacon'.

Bruce Kent and the Campaign for Nuclear Disarmament for an extract from a fundraising letter.

Cambridge University Press for extracts from *Something to Read* (1988) by C. Lindop and D. Fisher, *Authentic Reading* (1982) by C. Walter, *Interactive Approaches to Second Language Reading* (1988) by P. Carrell, J. Devine, and D. Esky (eds.), and *Learning to Learn English: A Course in Learner Training* (1989) by G. Ellis and B. Sinclair.

Cassell Ltd for extracts from *Advanced International English* (1989) by N. Brieger and A. Jackson.

China National Publishing Corporation for an extract from *Communicative English for Chinese Learners* (1986) by Xu Guozhang.

De Jager–Haum publishers, Pretoria, South Africa, and the Molteno Project for an extract from *Bridge Plus One: Pupils' Book* (1987).

The English Centre for an extract from *Changing Stories (1984)* by B. Mellor, J. Hemmings, and J. Leggett, *Reading Stories* (1987) by B. Mellor, M. O'Neill, and A. Patterson, and *Making Stories* (1984) by B. Mellor and M. Raleigh with P. Ashton.

Heinemann Educational Books for extracts from *Reasons for Reading* (1979) by E. Davies and N. Whitney.

Longman Group UK for extracts from *The Whole Story* (1988) by R. Rossner, *Advanced Reading Skills* (1981) by P. Barr, J. Clegg, and C. Wallace, *Contrasts: Developing Text Awareness* (1990) by D. Foll, and *Widely Read* and *Beneath the Surface* (1989) by S. Eckstut and D. Lubelska.

Macmillan Publishers Ltd for extracts from *Rice and Peas* (1975) by B. Gilroy, and *Reading in the Language Classroom* (1984) by E. Williams.

Marxism Today for three interviews by C. Granlund published in the June, August, and October 1989 issues.

The Ministry of Education, Jordan, for extracts from *New Living English for Jordan* (1970) by W. Stannard-Allen, M. El-Anani, and Y Salah.

Nelson Ltd for an exercise from *Shades of Meaning* (1983) by M. Ellis and P. Ellis.

Oxford University Press and R. Tomlinson and R. Ellis for an extract from *Reading: Advanced* (1988).

Oxford University Press (Delhi) for an extract from *Druk Readers Book Four* (1982) by D. Horsburgh.

Pelonis Inc. for permission to use the advertisement 'Cold War Ends'.

The Questor's Theatre for permission to reproduce their logo and a letter.

The Spastics Society for permission to reproduce artwork from a fundraising appeal.

Untuk Sekolah Menengah Atas Departmen Pendidikan dan Kebudayaan for an extract from *Bahasa Inggris* (1988) by M. Simatupang and A. Aryanto.

Zimbabwe School Readers Series for the poem by P. Dube from *Young Voices* (1986).